TWAYNE'S WORLD AUTHORS SERIES
A Survey of the World's Literature

GERMANY

Ulrich Weisstein, Indiana University
EDITOR

Klaus Mann

TWAS 435

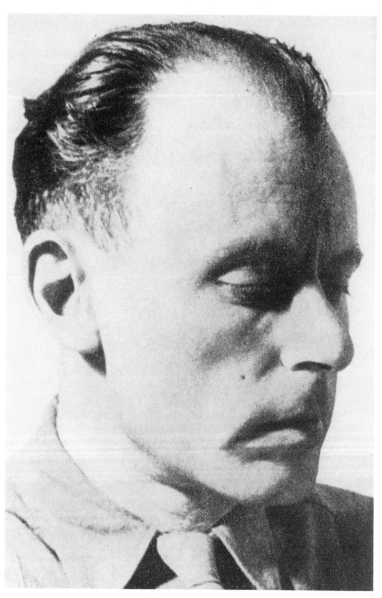

Klaus Mann

KLAUS MANN

By PETER T. HOFFER

Lincoln University

TWAYNE PUBLISHERS

A DIVISION OF G. K. HALL & CO., BOSTON

Library of Congress Cataloging in Publication Data

Hoffer, Peter T   1942–
  Klaus Mann.

  (Twayne's world authors series ; TWAS 435 : Germany)
  Bibliography: p. 143–46.
  Includes index.
  1. Mann, Klaus, 1906–1949.   2. Authors, German—
20th century—Biography.
PT2625.A435Z7   833'.9'12   77–22472
ISBN 0–8057–6309–0

Contents

About the Author

Peter T. Hoffer was born on May 27, 1942 in Providence, Rhode Island. He attended Columbia University, where he received his B.A. in 1964. He received his M.A. in German from Tufts University in 1965 and his Ph.D. in German from the University of Pennsylvania in 1975. Since 1971 he has been on the faculty of Lincoln University, where he is presently an Assistant Professor of German. Among his works being readied for publication are an article entitled "Klaus Mann and the Kaspar Hauser Complex" and a translation of a novella by Adolf Douai, a German-American Abolitionist and journalist. Professor Hoffer has also begun work on a translation of a book entitled *Ein Blick in die neue Welt* by Wilhelm Liebknecht, a prominent nineteenth century German Socialist.

Preface

This monograph is the first comprehensive critical-analytical study of Klaus Mann in English. It is intended for the reader who wishes to become acquainted with the work of this relatively unknown writer, as well as for the serious student of modern literature. References are to the latest editions of Klaus Mann's work, which are edited by Martin Gregor-Dellin and published by the *Nymphenburger Verlagshandlung* in Munich. In the case of those works which have not recently been reprinted, references are to the latest reprint or to the original edition.

Klaus Mann was both a writer of fiction and a literary and social critic. For the purpose of this study, emphasis has been placed on the interpretation of his fiction, with reference to his literary and social criticism primarily as it applies to his creative writing. Many of his political essays and pieces of literary criticism are not dealt with, simply because they have no direct bearing on his fiction, and limitations of space preclude their being treated here. Although certain unpublished manuscripts, such as those relating to the last years of the author's life, have been considered, other works such as *Revue zu Vieren* and *Geschwister*, which are out of print and not generally available, have been passed over.

In general, biographical details are limited to those which bear directly on the genesis of specific works. Klaus Mann's fiction has strong autobiographical elements which figure prominently in both plot and characterization. Throughout this study, effort has been made to point out where these elements are to be found and how they relate to Klaus Mann's life. While Klaus Mann was acquainted with many individuals of literary and historical significance, special consideration has been given to those whose direct influence on his work has been greatest. These include members of his immediate family, especially his father, Thomas Mann, his mother, Katja, and his sister, Erika. Some of the people with whom Klaus was associated to varying degrees of intimacy have been treated in connection with the writing or the publication of specific works; the vast majority of individuals with whom he came in contact during the course of his life, either casually or with some degree of intimacy, have been excluded from consideration.

Klaus Mann is best known for the books which he wrote during the period of his exile from Germany between 1933 and 1945. The number of his works published between 1925, when he had barely passed through adolescence, and 1933, when he was still a young man, is at least as large as that published during the remainder of his life. In order to present a balanced, coherent picture of his entire literary career, as much emphasis has been placed on his early, experimental work as on his mature writings. Where appropriate, biographical details have been used to elucidate certain works, and certain inferences about the author's life and personality have been made from his works. The result is, I hope, a study which will shed some light on Klaus Mann's development both as a writer and as a man.

Lincoln University, Pennsylvania   PETER T. HOFFER

Acknowledgments

There are many people to whom I am indebted for assisting me in the writing of this volume. My thanks go to Professors Frank Trommler, André von Gronicka, and the late Adolf Klarmann of the University of Pennsylvaia, whose advice helped solve some of the problems encountered in the initial stages of this undertaking. For his assistance and cooperation in securing many of Klaus Mann's unpublished manuscripts cited in this study, I thank Richard Lemp, curator of the manuscript collection of the *Stadtbibliothek* in Munich. I am also grateful to Dr. Hans Wysling, director of the Thomas Mann Archive of the Eidgenössische Technische Hochschule, Zurich, for assisting me in gaining access to some unpublished letters of Thomas Mann to his eldest son.

I am especially indebted to Professor Michael Mann of the University of California at Berkeley for his willingness to converse with me about his brother Klaus on July 19, 1972; and to Frau Katja Mann, who graciously invited me into her house at *Kilchberg am Zürichsee* on June 27, 1973 for an hour of delightful reminiscences about Klaus. I am also grateful to Peter de Mendelssohn, an old friend and former schoolmate of Klaus Mann, for some valuable insights into Klaus's early life.

I am grateful to Mr. Emery Wimbish and the staff of Langston Hughes Memorial Library of Lincoln University for their cooperation and their assistance in obtaining many of the materials needed for this study. Finally, I would like to extend thanks to all my friends and colleagues on the faculty of Lincoln University for their support and encouragement during the time it took to complete this project.

Chronology

1906   Klaus Mann is born on November 18, in Munich.

1910- Mann family spends summers in their country house in Bad
1918   Tölz, Bavaria. Experiences there provide background for Klaus's story, *Kindernovelle*.

1914   In January the Mann family moves to the house on the Poschingerstrasse in Munich, where they remain until 1933.

1915   Klaus undergoes emergency operation for appendicitis, which almost costs him his life.

1916   Klaus enters *Wilhelmsgymnasium* in Munich.

1919   February 21, Kurt Eisner, Bavarian Premier, is assassinated. Communist dictatorship in Munich. Klaus forms amateur theatrical group with his sister Erika and his friend Ricki Hallgarten.

1922   In March, Klaus and Erika enter the *Bergschule Hochwaldhausen*. In September, Klaus enters the *Odenwaldschule*.

1923   In November, Klaus returns to Munich, where he receives instruction from a private tutor.

1924   Engagement to Pamela Wedekind. Klaus is guest of Baron von Bernus at *Stift Neuburg*. Publishes first essays, anonymously, for *Die Weltbühne*. Writes theater reviews for *Zwölfuhrmittagsblatt* in Berlin.

1925   Organizes theater ensemble with Erika, Pamela, and Gustaf Gründgens. First performances of *Anja und Esther* in Munich and Hamburg. *Vor dem Leben* published.

1926   Publishes first novel, *Der fromme Tanz*.

1927- Travels to America and Asia with Erika. Trip is described in
1928   their book, *Rundherum*.

1929   Interest in politics intensifies. Becomes exposed to Pan-Europeanism of Count Coudenhove-Kalergi. Thomas Mann wins Nobel Prize.

1930   *Alexander* published. September 14, the National Socialists win one hundred and seven seats in the *Reichstag* elections.

1932   *Kind dieser Zeit* and *Treffpunkt im Unendlichen* published.
1933   March 13, Klaus emigrates from Germany. Edits *Die Sammlung* in Amsterdam. Erika founds *Pfeffermühle* in Zurich.
1934   January 11, Klaus loses his German citizenship. Takes part in the International Writers' Congress in Moscow. *Flucht in den Norden* published.
1935   *Symphonie Pathétique* published. Klaus visits his parents in Küsnacht bei Zürich, Switzerland. Temporary residence in Paris and the South of France.
1936   *Mephisto* published.
1937   Emigrates to the United States. Travels to Vienna, Prague, and Budapest. Lecture tour of the United States. Compiles material for a book about European emigrants, *Escape to Life*.
1938   Travels with Erika to Spain to report on Spanish Civil War.
1939   *Der Vulkan* published. Writes *The Other Germany* in collaboration with Erika.
1941   Edits the periodical *Decision* in New York. Begins work on *The Turning Point*.
1942   Begins writing *André Gide and the Crisis of Modern Thought*. May 28, completes final chapter of *The Turning Point*. December 14, accepted into the United States Army.
1943   January 6, inducted into the army at Fort Dix, New Jersey. Undergoes basic training at Camp Joseph T. Robinson, Arkansas; is transferred to Camp Ritchie, Maryland. Edits Camp Crowder, (Missouri) newspaper, "The Message." September 25, becomes naturalized United States citizen.
1944   Goes overseas as an American soldier. Tour of duty in North Africa and Italy. Assigned to the Psychological Warfare Branch of Military Intelligence.
1945   Becomes staff writer for *Stars and Stripes*. Returns to Germany as a correspondent after the war.
1946   Writes *Der siebente Engel*.
1948   July 11, attempts suicide in Santa Monica, California.
1949   May 21, commits suicide in Cannes.

CHAPTER 1

Introduction: Klaus Mann's Life and Work

KLAUS Mann was born on November 18, 1906 as the eldest son of Thomas and Katja Mann, one year after their daughter, Erika. He was a precocious, highly imaginative child, who soon developed an intimate relationship with his older sister, which very early began to stimulate the creative abilities of both children and was the beginning of an almost lifelong artistic collaboration. Together with their younger brother and sister, Golo and Monika, Klaus and Erika developed a repertoire of theatrical games which they shared with their elders and anyone else who was willing to observe them. Klaus displayed the greatest affinity for the written word, composing short plays, novelettes, and poems from a very early age.

Klaus's enthusiasm for formal education was inversely proportional to his creative potential. After being taught by a number of private tutors, he and Erika entered the *Volksschule* (elementary school), and later the *Wilhelmsgymnasium*, the German equivalent of high school, where Klaus's lack of interest in academic subjects caused his parents concern. At the age of sixteen, he was sent to the *Bergschule Hochwaldhausen*, a private country school; and shortly thereafter he transferred to the *Odenwaldschule*, a well-known progressive boarding school designed to accommodate highly gifted but difficult children. He became acquainted with its founder and headmaster, Paulus Geheeb, with whom he maintained contact for the rest of his life.

After spending about a year at the *Odenwaldschule*, Klaus returned to Munich, where he was instructed for a short time by a private tutor, and where he organized an amateur literary and theatrical group with Erika and some of his friends. Among these was

Pamela Wedekind, daughter of the famous playwright, Frank Wedekind. Klaus and Pamela became engaged, but the wedding never took place. In the spring of 1924, Klaus was a guest of Baron Alexander von Bernus, an acquaintance of his father, who owned a castle called Stift Neuburg, situated near the Neckar River, in Heidelberg. It was there that he wrote the *Kaspar Hauser Legenden*, which form the core of his first published work, *Vor dem Leben* (Before Life).

Late in 1924, at the age of eighteen, Klaus moved to Berlin, where he found a position writing theater reviews for a prominent local newspaper, the *Zwölfuhrmittagsblatt*. He had already published three anonymous critical essays for the periodical *Die Weltbühne*, but word leaked out that they had been written by the son of Thomas Mann. The event marked the beginning of a public attitude toward his work which unavoidably associated him with his father and was to be a lifelong source of concern and frustration. The press, which was never fully sympathetic to him, took every opportunity to subject him to ridicule. In reference to his engagement to Pamela, which received more than its share of publicity, Klaus wrote, "The sensationalistic maliciousness of the press made a bad and loud joke out of the fact that we wanted to marry. Pamela, Erika, and I: this bond, which seemed indestructible to us for so long, was perhaps the most beautiful and promising constellation in our lives."[1]

The constellation was still further consolidated when the three youngsters organized a theater ensemble which was joined by Gustaf Gründgens, who later became Erika's husband. The four collaborated in the production of Klaus's first play, *Anja und Esther*, which was performed in Hamburg, Munich, and Berlin. The following year, they went on tour with another play by Klaus entitled *Revue zu Vieren*, (Four in Revue), which received generally unfavorable reviews. Gründgens, relatively unknown at the time, later became a popular actor in Hamburg and went on to become the director of the German National Theater during the Third Reich. He and Erika were divorced, and Gründgens became the model for the main character in Klaus's novel *Mephisto*, a bitter attack on the excesses of National Socialism, which was published in 1936.

In the spring of 1926, Klaus journied to Paris, where he stayed for several months. There he met and befriended the young French writer René Crevel who was writing a novel entitled *La Mort Difficile* (The Difficult Death). Crevel's character served as a model for the hero of Klaus's next work, *Kindernovelle,* (Children's Novella), which was also based, in part, on Klaus's childhood experiences in the Mann's summer residence in Bad Tölz, Bavaria. Klaus's experiences in Berlin, Hamburg and Paris also provided background material for his first novel, *Der fromme Tanz*, published in 1926.

Klaus never lost the desire to travel. In 1927, when Pamela Wedekind broke their engagement and decided to marry the Expressionist playwright, Carl Sternheim, Klaus accepted an invitation to visit the United States from his friend Horace Liveright, who had published the English version of *Kindernovelle*, called *The Fifth Child*. By clever subterfuge, Klaus found a way to take Erika along on what was to become a much longer journey, one that would take the pair around the world in the next two years. It was Klaus's first exposure to American life; and he was able to meet a number of prominent literary and theatrical figures, many of German extraction, who made an indelible, if not entirely favorable impression on him. His feelings about American culture are reflected in an unpublished play, written in 1929, called *Gegenüber von China* (Across from China), which recounts the experiences of a European student who becomes disillusioned by American life during her stay at a small West Coast college. A short story by the same name, also written in 1929, satirizes the American success ethic by depicting a young man who goes to great lengths in order to secure a role in a Hollywood film. The entire world tour, which took Klaus and Erika across Asia and the Soviet Union, is described in their travel book, *Rundherum* (Roundabout).

In 1930, Klaus published *Alexander,* a historical novel about the great Macedonian conqueror. Klaus had already evidenced an interest in politics with the publication of such essays as *Fragment von der Jugend* (Fragment of Youth) and *Heute und morgen* (Today and Tomorrow), which expressed his concern about the direction which youth should take in influencing the course of contemporary events. In a monumental three-part essay entitled *Zur Situation* (About the Situation), written in 1930, he anticipated the clash between radical-leftist and reactionary forces which signalled the ascendancy of National Socialism; and he discussed ways in which the members of his generation could meet the crisis. It was

Klaus's dream one day to see a united Europe in which the narrow, divisive, nationalistic concerns of the individual states would be replaced by a more stable, unified political structure. While *Alexander* is not a political novel, its almost lyrical portrayal of the youthful conqueror, struggling to bring all the warring states of the world together under a single banner, is symbolic of his intense desire to witness a similar, though peaceful occurrence in his own time.

In 1932, Klaus wrote the first of his two autobiographies, *Kind dieser Zeit* (Child of this Time). It describes his experiences from his early childhood through his decision to take up residence in Berlin in 1924. In addition to giving insight into his early family relationships and the beginnings of his development as a writer, the book contains a lighthearted account of his adventures as a child and early adolescent and a sensitive analysis of the total meaning of childhood. In the same year, Klaus also completed a novel, *Treffpunkt im Unendlichen* (Meeting Point in Infinity), which consists of a series of episodes in the lives of a number of disparate characters who live in several major European cities and whose destinies are loosely interwoven. The end of the novel contains a scene with the two main protagonists which matches in almost every detail an experience with hashish which Klaus and Erika had in Fez, Morocco, and which is described in detail in Klaus's second autobiography, *Der Wendepunkt* (The Turning Point).[2] The novel contains many other autobiographical references as well.

On March 13, 1933, Klaus left Germany, not to set foot on German soil again until the end of the Second World War. His decision to emigrate at that time was not forced upon him by Nazi opposition to his political views, but was prompted by his almost physical revulsion to the events which were occurring in his homeland. Because of his left-wing leanings, his uncle Heinrich was the first member of the Mann family to be blacklisted by the Nazis. Erika, who had founded *Die Pfeffermühle (The Peppermill),* a satirical anti-Nazi cabaret in Zurich, was also officially expatriated, but her marriage to W. H. Auden enabled her to obtain a British passport. Klaus lost his German citizenship early in 1934, primarily because of his editorship of the vehemently anti-Fascist monthly, *Die Sammlung*, which was published in Amsterdam. Thomas Mann, who remained in Switzerland after the Nazi takeover, was last to receive the official condemnation of the Third Reich, after finally aligning himself with the exiles in 1936.

The first novels which Klaus wrote in Exile are *Flucht in den Norden* (English version: *Journey into Freedom*) and *Symphonie Pathétique*, a fictionalized account of the last years in the life of Peter Ilyitch Tchaikovsky. The former, published in 1934, is the story of a young, politically conscious woman, who, torn between her love for a man and her sense of allegiance to her threatened homeland, renounces love in favor of duty. It is Klaus Mann's first novel in which political exile is a major theme. The journey through Finland, from which the work takes its title, is based on a similar trip which Klaus and Erika made in 1931.

Symphonie Pathétique is a biographical novel, strongly resembling *Alexander* in conception. As in the latter, Klaus's main objective was not to maintain historical accuracy, but to convey as succinctly as possible the inner conflict which exists in a great individual at the peak of his creative potential. The composer, depicted in the process of completing his Sixth Symphony, is a man in almost constant torment, wracked by doubts and fears whose intensity is proportional to the greatness of the work. Tchaikovsky is consistently presented as an emotional exile, a man who hated to travel but whose circumstances required him to be almost constantly on the move, an artist who was able to compose the most exquisite music but in the final analysis was incapable, as a man, of creating harmony within himself.

After *Die Sammlung* ceased publication at the end of 1934, largely for financial reasons, Klaus once again began to travel through various parts of free Europe, taking up temporary residence either with his parents in Switzerland, or in Paris, or in the South of France. In 1936 he wrote *Mephisto*, which was to become perhaps his best-known work because of the controversy surrounding its main character, who closely resembles Gustaf Gründgens, Klaus's former brother-in-law. Although Klaus maintained that his purpose in writing the book was not to subject Gründgens to ridicule but to use him as a vehicle for exposing the excesses of the Third Reich, his attempts to have the novel republished in Germany after the Second World War were thwarted up to the end of his life, and even thereafter.[3]

Although Klaus had been granted a passport by the government of Czechoslovakia and was technically a Czech citizen, he returned to the United States late in 1936, eventually to settle in California. He returned to Europe briefly in February, 1937, visiting Prague,

Vienna, and Budapest, where he delivered lectures and interviewed a number of prominent political figures, among them the recently elected second president of Czechoslovakia, Edward Benes. Back in the United States once again, he was given a contract to travel across the country lecturing. Erika, who had had an unsuccessful debut of *The Peppermill* in New York, joined him. As relatively well-known German exiles, Klaus and Erika found themselves in the position of wanting to educate the American people about the evils of Nazism while at the same time having to defend the basic integrity of the German national character. Between 1937 and 1940, they jointly published two books: *Escape to Life* (1939), a series of informative sketches about prominent German exiles; and *The Other Germany* (1940), an attempt to consolidate the views about the political nature of Germany expressed in their lecture tours. Klaus's long-cherished idea of a federated Europe, to be constructed after the inevitable war with Germany, reemerges here.

In 1938, Klaus and Erika went to Spain to observe and report on the Spanish Civil War. While Klaus was not a Communist, he was a strong supporter of the Loyalist struggle and applauded at every turn the heroic efforts of the International Brigade in what he soon recognized was a lost cause. He was appalled by the vast destruction which he witnessed, brought about largely by the efforts of the expanding German war machine, which was using Spain as a testing ground for its newly developed techniques of aerial warfare. Klaus and Erika had the opportunity to interview a pair of Nazi pilots who had been shot down and taken prisoner by the Loyalists. Klaus had nothing but contempt for the glib manner with which they denied being aware that they had dropped their bombs on innocent women and children.

In 1939, Klaus published *Der Vulkan*, his longest and most ambitious novel. The "volcano" of the title refers to the world political situation, which in 1939 was on the verge of erupting into war. Klaus likened the situation of the German exiles to living on the slopes of a volcano, with the choice of either fleeing to safety in the distance or remaining helplessly to face the catastrophe and its inevitable consequences. The novel borrows its main structural elements from Klaus's earlier novels of emigration and from *Treffpunkt im Unendlichen*, with its network of loosely connected plots which unfold simultaneously. It contains a host of major characters whose common attribute is their exile and whose destinies are played out in various cities with which Klaus had become intimately acquainted: Paris, Amsterdam, Zurich, and New York. As in his earlier fiction, many of the characters have clearly discernible autobiographical traits. Martin Korella, who bears close resemblance to the author, is a frustrated writer who becomes addicted to morphine and dies, leaving his life's work, a historical narrative about the emigration, unfinished.

In 1941, Klaus moved to New York City, where he founded and edited a literary monthly, *Decision*, which he hoped would become not simply another organ for European writers in exile to air their views in, but a journal of the highest literary caliber as well. During the short span of its existence, which encompassed little more than a year, *Decision* was able to fulfill its promise. Klaus succeeded in gaining the wholehearted support of Thomas Mann, who not only helped secure financial backing for the journal but also contributed his own articles. In addition to receiving articles from prominent European writers in exile, *Decision* also printed contributions from distinguished British and American literary figures such as W. H. Auden, Sherwood Anderson, Stephen Vincent Benét, Somerset Maugham, Stephen Spender, and many others. The journal finally succumbed to financial pressures early in 1942, after repeated unsuccessful attempts on Klaus's part to solicit funds from wealthy potential backers who expressed interest in the venture but always stopped short of offering sufficient monetary support. Despite its brief existence, *Decision* stands as a monument to Klaus Mann's efforts and as an important document of the influence of the European intellectuals in America at the start of the Second World War.

In December, 1942, Klaus was inducted into the United States Army, after his application for enlistment had been repeatedly rejected by his draft board. He was eager to take an active part in the struggle against world Fascism, now as a soldier and not simply as a detached observer, as he had been for so many years. He was inducted at Fort Dix, New Jersey and was transferred to a number of military training camps in various parts of the United States. At Camp Crowder, Missouri, he edited the camp newspaper, "The Message." He was quickly promoted to the rank of Staff Sergeant and became a naturalized citizen in September, 1943, just before he received his orders to go overseas. He landed in North Africa and travelled with the Fifth Army to Italy, where, as a member of the Psychological Warfare Branch of Military Intelligence, he was frequently at the front distributing propaganda leaflets or using a loudspeaker to urge the German troops to surrender. In February, 1945, he became a staff writer for *Stars and Stripes,* the official newspaper of the American Armed Forces, for which he wrote numerous articles about German problems. In May, 1945, he entered Germany for the first time since his hasty departure in 1933 and was able to visit the ruins of his family home in Munich, which served as a poignant example of the devastation to which the entire country had been subjected. During his brief sojourn in post-war Germany, Klaus took the opportunity to interview a number of prominent Germans, among them Hermann Göring, Richard Strauss, and Emil Jannings.

The period following Klaus's discharge from the United States Army on September 28, 1945, marks the beginning of a general decline in his emotional well-being as well as his productivity. During the war, he had written little more than a few short stories and the articles which he produced as a writer for *Stars and Stripes.* Before his enlistment, he had completed his second autobiography, *The Turning Point*, and a biographical study of André Gide entitled *André Gide and the Crisis of Modern Thought.* With his friend Hermann Kesten, he had also edited an anthology of modern European creative writing entitled *Heart of Europe.* In 1946, he wrote a play, *Der siebente Engel* (The Seventh Angel), which he attempted unsuccessfully to have produced in Vienna. He had hoped that Helene Thimig, former wife of the renowned German director Max Reinhardt, would play the leading role. The play, a surrealistic comedy set on an island off the coast of California, bears many similarities to his early story, *Kindernovelle.* Highly imaginative and well structured, with its unique combination of autobiographical material and contemporary symbolism, it is a significant departure from his realistic, politically-centered prose of the pre-war era. Although its European performance rights were maintained by the Oprecht publishing house in Zurich, it was never published or performed and is the last major work of fiction which Klaus Mann completed in his lifetime.

On July 11, 1948, Klaus attempted to commit suicide in his apartment in Santa Monica, California. The press, which had always treated significant events in his life with the insensitivity which it customarily reserves for the offspring of famous people, was no more tactful than usual in this instance. Every sordid detail of the event was conscientiously described in the local newspapers. His family and close friends, however, were not completely surprised by the act; for they sensed that Klaus's mood and self-esteem had been gradually deteriorating since his return from the army. His brother Golo writes, "What I *felt*: my brother's soul was sick. The motor didn't want to run any more. I felt it already in the winter of '47, when we lived in an old-fashioned New York hotel by the name of 'Sevilla,' which has certainly long since disappeared. Again the political conversations as in the 1930's, but now completely without hope. There you had it, Klaus said. They, the Americans, would kill us all; all 'intellectuals,' everyone who had been for President Roosevelt and against Hitler. *That* was the war's true fruit."[4]

On May 21, 1949, less than a year after his earlier attempt, Klaus committed suicide in Cannes, France. Ironically, but hardly by coincidence, he had been working on a novel entitled *The Last Day,* about a man who kills himself in a fit of despondency over the unfavorable post-war political situation. Although political factors partly account for his final desperate act, they do not, in and of themselves, satisfactorily explain it. The fact that he had not published a major work in several years and was encountering difficulties in finding a market in Germany for his earlier works were also contributing factors. He had no money when he died. He and Erika were no longer as close as they had been in earlier years. His basic circumstances, however, were not radically different from what they had been for most of his adult life. He had lived for so many years as an exile, not simply from his homeland, but from the people who were closest to him; during his life he had made many personal contacts but formed few meaningful relationships. His death provided a way of altering this pattern.

CHAPTER 2

The Early Years

I First Literary Attempts

THE urge to write made its appearance early in Klaus's life. One of his earliest poems, written in collaboration with his sister Erika, is quoted in his first autobiography, *Kind dieser Zeit*. It was, by Klaus's own estimate, written at the age of six:

> Der böse Mörder Gulehuh,
> Der jagte eine bunte Kuh
> Die bunte Kuh, die sträubt sich sehr
> Der Gulehuh kriegt das Messer her.
> Er haut der Kuh das Köpfchen ab,
> Der Bauer kommt daher im Trab.
> Er hat den Gulehuh eingefangen,
> in drei Tagen soll er am Galgen hangen . . .

(The wicked murderer Gulehuh chased a motley cow. The motley cow resists strongly. Gulehuh takes the knife. He knocks the cow's head off. The farmer comes trotting up. He has caught Gulehuh. In three days he'll hang from the gallows . . .") If Klaus's memory served him correctly, the sample is indeed the product of a gifted and precocious mind. The choice of words, the rhyme, and the uniformity of meter indicate a facility with language which far exceeds what one would expect from a six-year-old. Nor is this poem an isolated example. The quantity of Klaus's early writings, many of which were preserved by the author himself, is staggering: "In the quickest tempo there originated that quantity of dramas, novels, sketches, and ballads, almost all of which I have saved, and the mass of which frightens me so much." (*Kind*, p. 33)

Much of Klaus's early creative work was done with the active participation of Erika, one year his senior and the eldest of the six

Mann children. The spiritual bond between the two was unusually close and was to remain so well into their adult lives. The early fantasy life which developed between them, and which Klaus so aptly describes as he traces the origins of his literary productivity, assumed a particularly intense and complex character. They developed a "secret" language, consisting of words and phrases whose meaning only they could understand:

> The word "üsis" played an enormous role in our vocabulary (and it still does so today). Its origin and meaning are not easy to explain. Originally derived from "putzig" and developing over "usig" to its final form "üsis," it was first applied to dolls and animals. In a vague and gentle way it designated everything which affected us in an awkward, moving, forced, wide-eyedly droll, clumsily congenial manner . . . The antonyms to üsis were "wuffig" on the one hand, "klie-klie" on the other. (*Kind*, pp. 30-31)

The fact that this particular aspect of their relationship remained virtually unchanged from its original appearance in early childhood and that it lasted well into their adult lives is particularly significant in light of their continued personal and artistic collaboration, which remained intact even during the period of their exile from Germany and did not begin to dissolve until Klaus's entry into the American army at the start of World War II. It could also account, in part, for the numerous women in Klaus's work up to that time who bear a resemblance to Erika Mann.

A relatively late manifestation of this type of intimacy between the two siblings occurred around 1927 in Hollywood, during their much-publicized round-the-world tour, which was described in detail in the book *Rundherum* (Roundabout), on which they also collaborated. After witnessing a performance of the play "Dracula," Klaus and Erika were much impressed by its sadistic theme: an innocent girl, "Miss Lucy," ostensibly being treated for an unnamed degenerative disease by a doctor in the employ of the famous Count Dracula, is actually supplying an ample source of blood for the count's unnatural appetite. As the unfortunate girl grows weaker because of her daily loss of blood, the cruel doctor, feigning concern for the patient's welfare, would greet her daily with the words, "Our poor Miss Lucy looks very tired this morning."[2] Klaus and Erika adopted this phrase with all of its bizarre associations and used it on numerous occasions when they were in embarrassing or otherwise difficult situations which required some lessening of tension. The phrase became something of a leitmotif in their lives: "Our agent made every effort to arrange a lecture tour for us, but made no real progress. Now and then we would visit the good man in his office, whereupon it occurred to us that his demeanor each time became more and more concerned. 'Our poor Miss Lucy!' we whispered to each other, full of sympathy. 'She looks very very tired again!' " (*Wendepunkt*, p. 185). And, at a point when they had run out of money and did not have enough to pay the hotel bill:

"And how is the patient now?" whispered my sister in her best Dracula accent, as soon as the fiend [the hotel-keeper] had left us alone.
"My dear Miss Lucy," I answered, earnestly but composed. "There is only one thing to do: We must sit down together and make a plan." (*Wendepunkt*, p. 191)

The air of theatricality exemplified here apparently persisted between brother and sister and was to continue to appear on numerous subsequent occasions. It was indicative of a much broader complex of relations which existed for most of their lives and made itself apparent in Klaus Mann's work in a number of different guises, which will be discussed in greater detail in the analysis of his individual works.

In addition to Erika, whose influence on Klaus was strongly rooted in early childhood and continued to exert a profound effect on both his personal and artistic life well beyond childhood and adolescence, there was another member of his immediate family whose early presence in his life exerted an equally profound effect on the development of his personality and his eventual decision to become a writer.

Mention has been made of Klaus's childhood literary endeavors. There can be no doubt that the image of his father, a writer who had already received world recognition before the birth of his eldest son, exerted a tremendous influence on young Klaus. Unquestionably, the talent which allowed him to write poems, plays, and novels before the age of fifteen, which, although of dubious literary merit, possessed a style and vocabulary worthy of any literate adult, preceded any direct influence his father might have had on his literary productivity. Perhaps because he was aware of this talent, Klaus did not see fit to credit Thomas Mann with inspiring any significant aspect of his early artistic endeavors. In attempting to analyze the source of his creative proclivities, he becomes characteristically abstract:

The need to write sets in before any content exists. The instinct to write operates as an end in itself, without reference to a moral or any other personal set of problems. There is nothing to confess (or if there is it remains inexpressible; the earliest adventures find their expression only much later): thus, this endless inventing *ex nihilo.* — Hence, if I have, at one time or another, stated that I never "invented" stories, that was a lie — or rather: it only applies to work done after my fifteenth year. Up to that time I simply thought up hundreds of stories out of the blue. (*Kind*, p. 33)

Regardless of how Klaus Mann attempted to explain the source of his creative penchant, it is certain that his fifteenth year was a pivotal stage in the development which led up to his decision to become a writer.

In describing the day-to-day relationship with his father, Klaus conveys the image of a man not given to tenderness, whose most frequent way of expressing affection for his children was largely the use of words lofty in import and pregnant with meaning. In fact, Thomas Mann for most of his life was bound to a strict work schedule which allowed him little room for flexibility. His children knew of their father's fame from an early age, and they soon grew accustomed to his way of life; yet they must have found the formal atmosphere of the household, along with their father's dour demeanor, trying at times:

Our father was more reserved and came less in contact with our day-to-day affairs. Instead, he had a strong suggestive power when he levelled his words at us or personally led an excursion (such as a visit to the theater). His utterings turned into classical quotations, simply because they were infrequent. Thus at the table, he would simply hand Erika—*only* Erika—a date and in so doing would explain this horrible arbitrariness to us as follows: "It is good for you to accustom yourselves to injustice at the proper time—" a remark, which we found to be amazingly frivolous and heartwarming at the same time. (*Kind*, p. 37)

Although Klaus was reluctant to acknowledge any special debt to his father for inspiring his literary activities, his manner of working and the intensity with which he followed the rigid work schedule which he set for himself throughout his productive life were similar in many respects. Many years later, shortly after Klaus's death, Thomas Mann was to write these words about his late son:

I also want to praise his industriousness, which was extraordinary. In relation to the short span of his existence and the restlessness of his life, the scope of his work is enormous. Wherever he came in his constant wandering, in every lodging or hotel room, the place was immediately set in good order for work: a few pictures hung, a few books shelved, photographs distributed, and he sat down at his typewriter. Such diligence is, in my opinion, something more than diligence itself.[3]

If there was any open conflict between father and son during his childhood and adolescence, Klaus gives little indication of it in his writings about these early stages of his life. In fact, on one of the few occasions on which he mentions the possibility of such an occurrence, he tends to minimize its importance:

The father-son conflict was present in my life for scarcely one year. I find it, as things are nowadays, to be the most superfluous and uninteresting of all problems. Every difference, every conflict today runs across the generations, not between the generations. The father is no longer the rigid conservative, the son the revolutionary (the relationship has rather reversed itself). (*Kind*, p. 229)

Although it appears as though whatever conflict may have existed between Klaus and Thomas Mann was resolved fairly early in the son's life, the behavior which will be explored presently and the feelings of inadequacy which were to plague him periodically for the remainder of his life, and which led to the suicidal depression which eventually destroyed him, are due, at least partly, to a continuing conflict with the image of his father which remained unresolved.

II   *Disorder and Early Sorrow*

In a chapter of *Kind dieser Zeit* entitled "Triumph der Bosheit" (Triumph of Evil), Klaus describes a series of adventurous pranks in which he and Erika engaged during their early adolescence. One of the many examples of this type of behavior which Klaus cites in his autobiography was their use of the telephone in making fraudulent calls to people of repute, sometimes causing them much incon-

venience. Evidence of such trickery (of a more innocuous and, perhaps, amusing nature) persisted beyond adolescence into early
adulthood. As a young writer in Berlin in 1924, Klaus had the opportunity to write theater reviews for the *Zwölfuhrmittagsblatt*, a
local newspaper. Since his critiques were written anonymously, he
found that he could indulge himself with total impunity in the most
exaggerated and insincere comments and thus derive secret pleasure
by deceiving "the dumb adults in the subway." (*Wendepunkt*,
p. 150) As he became older and more sure of himself, this mischie-
vous trait gradually weakened, but he never rid himself of it entirely, and some remnant of his early sadistic tendencies was always
present, even as an adult. Muriel Rukeyser, who befriended Klaus
when they were both working on the ill-fated periodical *Decision* in
the early 1940's, recalls that he once appeared at her door wearing a
rubber mask: "The laughter I remember when the despair was most
furious. When the masks of the dull and overblown crowded
around; when the drain of bills and commitments was most his
vampire; when the political scene could not be cut through by him;
when the painted faces of his dread were worst—then Klaus's
laughter, and his refusals."[4] The technique of applying fantasy and
humor as a defense against emotionally trying situations which he
and Erika had developed over the years was continued by Klaus
well into his mature years, even after the bond with Erika began to
grow weaker.

The period of Klaus's schooling was a trying and frustrating one
for him, characterized by many different and often opposing
moods. What is important for this discussion is that it was also a
time when the thematic and stylistic pattern of his writing began to
take shape. Throughout his relatively brief formal education, Klaus
showed little interest in the traditional course work which characterized the typical secondary school education in Germany during
the early 1900's; and his performance showed it. After spending
some time in the *Wilhelmsgymnasium* in Munich in his early teens,
he prompted his parents, through his lackluster performance,
finally to look about for other means of educating him. His overall
impression of the school, as he found it in 1916, reflects the bore-
dom and apathy which this experience must have generated in him:
"It is neither with hatred nor with feeling that I recall the old
Wilhelmsgymnasium, but only with bored indifference." (*Wendepunkt*, p. 74)

His parents cast about for other schools which might produce a spark of motivation in young Klaus, and in their search came upon two progressive schools which were to have a major impact on his development—although not in the way they hoped: the *Bergschule Hochwaldhausen* and the *Odenwaldschule*. The former was located in central Germany, in a region called the Rhön, not far from the town of Fulda. It was a country school, a *Landerziehungsheim*, founded on the principles of progressive education which were in vogue in Germany at that time; and it provided something of a respite for Klaus, a chance to get away from his parents. This was important for him in two respects: first, it gave him his first exposure to the *Jugendbewegung* (Youth Movement), which, although he did not participate wholeheartedly in its program, was to have a strong influence on the shaping of his subsequent views on the problems of contemporary youth; and second, it gave him the opportunity to be with Erika even more than before, since they were now attending the same school.

During the period of his schooling, the first indications of the overt homosexual tendencies which were later to become an intrinsic part of Klaus's life and work began to appear; and, although he never delved into that aspect of his life in any detail, there can be no doubt that it played a significant role in his entire makeup and significantly contributed to the problems which he was unable to surmount in later life. At the *Wilhelmsgymnasium*, he was sexually drawn to a boy named Elmar.

Elmar had silky-smooth, short, dark hair; sly, melancholy brown eyes and a smooth face. He was a very good gymnast. During the whole time in which I loved him—it was several months—I spoke hardly fifty words to him. Once I sent him one of the poems that I had made for him, anonymously and typewritten. I never found out what he thought of it, and I would still very much like to know. (*Kind*, p. 153)

And, in recounting his experience at *Hochwaldhausen,* he writes:

I fell in love several times, but not with the consuming ardor as in the case of Elmar or the one who awaited me in the Odenwaldschule. . . . The feeling never seized me totally and completely then; I could always accommodate it as a good and necessary factor in the puppet show of interwoven relations which I arranged for my own pleasure. (*Kind*, p. 174)

Early in 1922, Klaus informed his parents that he no longer wished to remain at *Hochwaldhausen*. After inspecting another, similar country school on Lake Constance with their mother, it was decided that Erika would return to Munich while Klaus would visit the *Odenwaldschule*, located near Heppenheim in the neighborhood of Heidelberg, founded and administrated by Paulus Geheeb, one of the most admired liberal educators of the time. Klaus, too, showed a great deal of respect for him; and he later became the model for the character, *"Der Alte"* (The Old One), in his first play, *Anja und Esther*, published in 1925.

The *Odenwaldschule*, was, in the words of Peter de Mendelssohn, "a school for very talented, difficult children," and "not an ordinary world."[5] Based on the same educational philosophy as *Hochwaldhausen*, and possessing a similar physical plant, it had a free curriculum, which enabled students to enroll in courses according to their ability rather than to take a fixed sequence of prerequisites. Klaus seemed to adapt quite well to the system there, although the strict routine of non-academic activities such as cold showers and kitchen-duty, more highly organized than at *Hochwaldhausen*, began to take its toll.

Despite the fact that, from all outward appearance, things seemed to be going as well as could be expected for Klaus, there was a certain air of malaise and discontent present beneath the surface of his seemingly placid spirit. During this time he was undergoing a kind of religious crisis, which manifested itself in his writing and behavior. He wrote a great deal in his spare time—chiefly poems of a religious or erotic nature inspired by readings of Nietzsche and George Trakl, among others. In writing about them later, he tended to criticize himself for these outpourings of feeling, prompted largely by guilt over adolescent excesses, but managed to find ways of justifying them: "But I know that certain moods in which I wrote down dithyrambic effusions and called them the 'flight of my soul to God,' were truly authentic—trance-states of a religious-erotic rapture." (*Kind,* p. 191)

Whether his feelings at this time were genuine or not, the "religious-erotic" aspects of his work are interesting from a psychological point of view, if not from a literary-critical one. An example of a religious poem:

Du hast mir grosse Demut gegeben, Herr —

Aber eitel blieb ich trotzdem.
Auch weiss ich, Herr, dass ich noch keine eigene
Sprache fand,
Zu dir zu beten—
Anderen,Grösseren, entlieh ich mein Gebet. (!) (*Kind*, p. 191)

("You have given me great humility, Lord—But despite this, I remained vain. I also know, Lord, that I have still not found my own
language, to pray to you—*From others, greater ones, I borrowed
my prayer.* (!)")
     And an erotic poem:

In deinem Haar ruh'n meine Hände aus.
Nach all dem vielen Suchen, all dem Tasten
Kam mich die Sehnsucht an, hier auszurasten—
In deinem Haar ruh'n meine Hände aus.

Verzeih, verzeih, wenn ich dir wehe tue—
In dieses Schicksal musst du dich bescheiden:
Von mir geliebt sein, heisst gar manches leiden.
Dennoch verzeih, wenn ich dir wehe tat. (*Kind*, p. 190)

("In your hair, my hands rest. After all the searching, all the touch-
ing, the yearning came over me to rest here. In your hair, my hands
rest. Forgive me, forgive me if I cause you pain—To this fate, you
must resign yourself. To be loved by me means much suffering.
Yet, forgive me If I caused you pain.") It is significant that the "religious" crisis revealed in these poems occurred simultaneously
with a sexual one. For an adolescent of sixteen, particularly one
who must live under such controlled and closely supervised conditions as those existing at the *Odenwaldschule*, burgeoning sexual
thoughts and feelings are at best difficult to handle, all the more so
since Klaus disdained any organized athletic activity, one of the
more effective ways of dealing with such conflicts. Instead, he did
an enormous amount of reading and was even exempted from some
classes when it was observed that his inclinations departed from
structured education toward a more independent mode of intellectual activity. Despite the fact that, in *Kind dieser Zeit*, Klaus describes these events after more than ten years, he gives little conscious indication that he was excessively troubled or unhappy during

this period, even though the facts as he depicts them seem to indicate the opposite.

In any event, the juxtaposition of mystical and religious feelings with eroticism was to continue to have a special meaning for him in later years and was destined to appear in many guises in his writing: "My relation to the landscape and to nature as a whole was determined by the mystic-erotic frame of mind in which I found myself: I embraced trees, I laid my face against their bark, and I felt the soft substance of the moss as a caress beneath the thin soles of my sandals." (*Kind*, p. 198)

Coupled with the tendency to eroticize his surroundings was a predilection for the baser, animalistic aspects of human nature, the treatment of which he, as a forthcoming writer, felt to be within his province. In 1918, at the age of thirteen, he wrote a novel called *Heinrich Hollmann, Geschichte einer Jugend* (Heinrich Hollmann, the Story of a Youth). In it he attempted to deal, through the medium of fiction, with a problem which had preoccupied him for some time:

In the story of this Heinrich—with whom I meant myself and whom I characterized with a certain malice—it was a question of a genuinely moral problem, in fact, of *the* moral problem par excellence: how man, as a spiritual-sensual dichotomy, is torn back and forth in a conflict between sensual pleasure and highest devotion to duty; how the animal in him vies with the god in him; the body with the mind; the indolent with the angelic. (*Kind*, p. 124)

The problem of mind versus body, soul versus flesh, is one which has continued to challenge the minds of philosophers and theologians down through the ages; but Klaus, as a burgeoning writer, chose to treat it in fictional form. What is significant in this early attempt, however, is the conscious link between the hero of the story and its author, a link which will be seen to persist in the portrayals of principal characters in his later works. Heinrich Hollmann finally dies of causes related to narcotics addiction, with the fatal conflict, which had raged in his soul for so long, still unresolved, ". . . a man, in whom the animal had emerged victorious, a restless, driven man, who scorned men and the immortal works of their civilization and loved them with the entire volcanic-animalistic force of his soul." (*Kind*, pp. 124-125)

In attempting to justify his choice of such a subject, Klaus sheds additional light on the relationship between his theme and his frame of mind at the time the work was written: "I could conceive of my own end only as in ruins and in sinful misery; I revelled in this idea—as a strong sympathy with a morally degrading, the lost, sinful, and decayed developed in me along with a penchant toward the moral theme, which I have retained and of which I am not ashamed: it is the other side of that deeper moral interest." (*Kind*, p. 125) In describing a story he wrote at the age of fifteen, called *Vorfrühling* (Before Spring), which has clear homosexual implications and whose main character is a boy named Elmar, Klaus talks of the secret pleasure he had in exposing the story to one of his teachers in the *Wilhelmsgymnasium:*

What, then, brought me to this shameful revelation?—On the one hand, ordinary vanity certainly came into play; on the other hand, the wish to disconcert and intimidate the principal, by providing him with a view into such a sick and sinfully melancholy world. . . . [It was] finally, however, quite simply that inborn *exhibitionism* which almost inevitably goes along with the phenomenon of artistic talent—or rather only with the urge for artistic self-representation; *the deep desire of every artistic man for scandal, for self-revelation.* . . . (*Kind*, p. 161)

The tendency to expose himself, to exhibit with minimal restraint the dark, unspeakable aspects of human life, while more or less characteristic of the artistic temperament in general, was to become a significant aspect of his art, more apparent in the early works, such as *Vor dem Leben*, but still palpably evident in the later works as well.

Early in 1923, Klaus returned to Munich in a surprise visit to his parents—an act which was not uncharacteristic of him, since he and Erika had developed the habit of taking trips to various places unbeknownst to their parents—and announced that he had had enough of the *Odenwaldschule* and wished to return to Munich. In the meantime he had developed a relationship with a boy named Uto, to whom he had inexplicably declared that it had been his parents' decision that he leave the *Odenwaldschule*. Since he had forfeited the right to return to the state school system, and his parents were still hoping to salvage some education for him, he was instructed for some months by a number of private tutors, who enjoyed little success in inspiring Klaus to achievement in their various subjects. By this time it became clear to everyone involved that Klaus would never be an academician and that his talents and inclinations were directed elsewhere. In February, 1924, as if acting on impulse, Klaus wrote a letter to his father—who was at the time in his study, two floors below Klaus in their house on the *Poschingerstrasse*—declaring his intention to start a new life as a dancer. This event transpired shortly after his first visit to Berlin, where he had made a whimsical and unsuccessful debut as an entertainer in a cabaret called "Tü-Tü".[6] He finally managed to convince his parents, by taking to his bed for a brief, unspecified period of time, that he was determined no longer to pursue his formal education, and that they should release him from the bondage of his hated tutor. He now had as much time as he wanted and managed to spend most of it in the company of his friends in Munich, among whom was Pamela Wedekind, the daughter of the famous playwright Frank Wedekind. He soon became engaged to her. They were both eighteen years old.

It was the era of inflation, but despite the difficult and unpredictable situation, the Mann family managed to remain financially solvent and did not undergo any undue hardship. Klaus, finally relieved of the onus of his studies, lived a life of comparative ease, socializing among his "*Münchner Freundeskries*" (Munich friends' circle)[7] and continuing his writing, which, by this time, comprised an essential part of his daily routine. He wrote what he called *Fromme Lieder* (Pious Songs), which he combined with his earlier religious poems to form a cycle. An example: "Es gibt im Grunde nur Gebete / so sind die Hände uns geweiht / Dass sie nichts schufen, was nicht flehte—" (*Kind*, p. 218). ("There are basically only prayers. So the hands are consecrated to us, in such a way that they created nothing which did not supplicate—") He also began to write political poems, which had much of the character of cabaret songs:

> Die jungen Proletarier
> Haben schwarze Sweater an
> Und eine schiefe Mütze
> Mit einer roten Nelke dran. (*Kind*, p. 219)

("The young proletarians are wearing black sweaters, and a slanted cap with a red carnation on it.")

Around this time Klaus, Erika, Pamela, and Walter Süskind founded a small cabaret, which allowed them, particularly Erika, to develop the theatrical talents which would be most fully exploited a few years later in Berlin and elsewhere. Some of their activities, however, assumed an almost orgiastic character, which continued to cause their parents concern. Most of the attempts to discipline the wayward youngsters were to no avail, however; Thomas Mann's efforts to assert his authority usually fell far short of their mark. Interestingly enough, it was the mother, Katja Mann, who exerted the most moderating influence on Klaus, retrieving him after some of his frequent attempts to flee the household and generally acting as something of a mediator between father and son. Despite the palpable "disorder" in Klaus's life after he left the *Odenwaldschule* and before he took up extended residence in Berlin to begin his career as a writer, this time of transition appears, by his account, to have been one of the relatively happy periods in his life. Two samples of his writing from this period are given in *Kind dieser Zeit*: the first, a poem, dedicated to his friend Uto, and the second, a fragment of a novella, which he never published. The poem, which contains many erotic elements, follows:

> So wie den Tod lieb' ich nur deine Hände.
> Nur deine Hände, mein geliebtes Kind,
> An die ich alle Zärtlichkeit verschwende,
> Die rauh und kindlich, ohne Makel sind.
>
> Was war der dunkle Ton, der in dein Weinen
> Sich mischte, und doch einem Jubel glich?
> Der Ton war's, den die Töne alle meinen,
> Es gibt auf dieser Welt nur diesen einen.
> Es gibt auf dieser Welt den Tod und dich—(*Kind*, p. 235)

("Like death, I love only your hands. Only your hands, my dear child, on which I squander all tenderness, which are rough and childlike, without blemish. What was the dark tone which mixed with your weeping, yet resembled a rejoicing? It was that tone which all tones mean. There is in this world only this one. There is in this world death and you.")

It bears a strong resemblance to the poem, "In deine Haarm ruh'n meine Hände aus," written while Klaus was at the *Odenwaldschule*. The emphasis on hands in both poems reflects Klaus's continued preoccupation with the "religious-erotic" perspective, and the association of love with death will appear many times in his subsequent work. Although it is difficult to assess whether Klaus had any serious thoughts about suicide during this period, he mentions obliquely that he ". . . played with the terrible and sweet idea of suicide." (*Kind*, p. 211)

The fragment is of considerable significance, both because it introduces a symbol which would figure prominently in the development of his work as a whole and because it reflects a situation which had a special meaning for him at that particular time in his life. To summarize it briefly, it is the story of a fifteen-year-old prince named Kaspar, who is being aided by his instructor in fleeing the monastic home of his strict father, the king. The name Kaspar bears a relation to the character Kaspar Hauser, who appears in the series of vignettes entitled *Kaspar Hauser Legenden*, in the volume, *Vor dem Leben*, Klaus's first published work. It was derived from a historical character of the early nineteenth century, a foundling of reputed noble birth, who was murdered by unknown assassins, and whose origins remain largely shrouded in mystery. Later taken up as a literary motif in a poem by Verlaine and a novel by Jakob Wassermann, Kaspar Hauser became a popular symbol of the times, representing the poor, innocent youth cast out of his home and about to enter an unsympathetic, hostile world. Kaspar is also one of the main characters of the play *Anja und Esther*, and was played by Klaus himself in the first performance. The relationship here between Prince Kaspar—and by implication the whole Kaspar-Hauser-complex, which figures prominently in Klaus's early work—and Klaus's own life situation is evident:

Precisely Prince Kaspar, strangest child of a strict and decorous monarch, deep at home in the quiet corridors of the monastically dark school, had to get away, no matter how much such slovenliness would anger the father. Victim of every desire and every desperation, he had either to be in the middle of life, *not being strong enough* to submerge himself in it and lose himself entirely; or he had to become lonelier, stronger, more himself than perhaps the dominating father, who, having matured not through sacrifice, but rather, by avoiding it, had made his way much too easily. (*Kind*, p. 237)

Klaus's own interpretation of the story offers many autobiographical references:

In the ascetic face of the educator . . . I recognize the traits of my teacher
Heinrich Sachs; the monastic institute is half a romantically altered country school, half another "foundation" which I would soon become acquainted with; it anticipates that mystical "sanitarium," from which later
the children in "Anja and Esther" would begin their departure into life.
The name Kaspar—which the autobiographical character in "Anja and
Esther" would also bear—shows the relation to the Kaspar-Hauser-
complex. (*Kind*, p. 239)

Klaus might have added that the description of "a strict and decorous monarch" closely fits that of Thomas Mann in his relationship
with his adolescent son of fifteen. Although Klaus does not analyze
his relations with his father at the time the work was conceived in
detail, he does refer once more to the "father-son conflict," the
significance of which he had earlier disavowed, in terms of its effect
on what he was trying to achieve as a writer:

The father-son opposition, alluded to here, is less prominent in the *Vor
dem Leben* volume, than it became later on, or it is much more strongly
stylized. Just at that time, as I was intellectually dependent on my father in
many things, I tried hard to work out those things in myself which I sensed
to be in opposition to him. While I became acquainted piece by piece with
"The Magic Mountain," which was nearing its end, and read all his earlier
works again and again, I tried to clarify in my mind what I would ever
have to pit against the closed block of this intellectual achievement. That is
why I loved to emphasize the Catholic before the Protestant; the pathetic
before the ironic; the plastic before the musical; the "deification of the
body" before the "sympathy with the abyss" . . . the extravagant, eccen-
tric, infamous, against the moderate; the irrationally intoxicated against
that which is contained and controlled by reason. (*Kind*, pp. 239-40)

While Klaus Mann may not have been aware of all the
implications of the influences which his early life and his relations
with family and friends during the crucial years of his adolescence
had on his work, as soon as he made the conscious decision to dedicate his life to becoming a writer the course of his artistic career had
been set. Although his first literary attempts are, in may respects,
rudimentary and lacking in the perspective which can only be
gained through a long and difficult process of personal and artistic
maturation, they contain the germs of ideas and motivations which
would find more articulate expression later on. What remains to be
seen is the extent to which these early influences manifested them-

selves as his artistic career progressed, how they changed with his changing life situation, and what effect new subsequent experiences may have had on his literary output.

CHAPTER 3

The Early Works: 1925-30

I Before Life: Kaspar Hauser Legenden

VOR dem Leben (Before Life) is the title of Klaus Mann's first published work, completed in 1925, while he was living in Berlin.[1] It is a collection of short stories written in a consciously neo-Romantic style which reflects his experimentation with certain subject matters and modes of expression before settling down to the more realistic style which would characterize his mature work. Most prominent among these are the *Kaspar-Hauser-Legenden* (Kaspar Hauser Legends), whose main character, as we have seen, assumed a special significance for the youthful Klaus Mann and warrants further investigation in light of his continued influence on the author's creative writings.

One of the main sources of the story of Kaspar Hauser is the novel by Jakob Wassermann, with which Klaus was thoroughly familiar, and which gives a most detailed description of the character and a complete account of his adventures. According to the novel, Kaspar Hauser first appeared as a foundling of seventeen, unable to speak because of a cruel and prolonged imprisonment, who was gradually brought back to a normal existence by the patient ministrations of a sympathetic teacher. Found to be of noble birth, but originally imprisoned so that a rival branch of his family could illegitimately assume power, he came under the tutelage of various benefactors, with whom he underwent a rigorous and often trying process of education. Finally, he was beset by enemies, who contrived a devious and elaborate plot to kill him, which eventually succeeded. On his tombstone were engraved the words: "Hic jacet Casperus Hauser, aenigma sui temporis, ignota nativitas, occulta mors."[2] (Here lies Caspar Hauser, enigma of his time, unknown birth, secret death). Wassermann's Caspar Hauser is basically a passive hero, who falls victim to circumstances over which he has little control and becomes increasingly withdrawn and suspicious of people as the course of his life unfolds. All through his privations he maintains an air of childish innocence, chastity, and naivité.

In June, 1925, Klaus Mann published a short article in the *Weltbühne* entitled "Kaspar Hauser," in which he set down his feelings after reading the Wassermann novel and expressed in considerable detail the intensely personal meaning which the figure conveyed to him:

When I read the book to the end for the first time and was thus freed from the hypnotizing magic of the epic narrative—I began to think, I tried, sitting there reflecting over the closed book, to explain to myself why this enigmatic youth's fate and history moved me so much, almost personally, and I soon recognized the similitude of his life, and that here, only emphasized through external circumstances, was made apparent to me through some coincidence a basically inner destiny that was very close to me, indeed, that was all too well known and long familiar to me. I connected the figure of the youth, which at that time had come to life for me, with many other things that I loved and with which I was bound up.[3]

In this passage, Klaus Mann asserts not only an intense emotional involvement with the figure of Kaspar Hauser, but he also strongly intimates that the character conveyed a meaning for him which was not merely aesthetic but which had a direct bearing on his life—a symbol, not only applicable to his art, but to the way in which he viewed his own lifestyle and the people who were intimately associated with it. It is thus important to view those artistic works of Klaus Mann with which the figure of Kaspar Hauser is associated not merely as expressions of a creative imagination, but as statements with a strong autobiographical component. It would be reasonable to expect that certain works which contain a figure which the author himself singles out as having "a basically inner destiny, that was very close to me, indeed, that was all too well known and long familiar to me . . ." would contain other aspects and features with which he was intimately acquainted.

As mentioned, Klaus Mann's artistic conception of Kaspar Hauser is reflected in the volume, *Vor dem Leben*, in a series of seven vignettes, and in a short introductory poem which serves as a motto for the whole. The vignettes are all written in the lyrical, dreamlike style characteristic of his early "Romantic" period. The first of these, also a poem, entitled "Kaspar Hauser Singt" (Kaspar

Hauser Sings), sets the tone for the remaining parts of the cycle.
Like many of the unpublished poems of Klaus's early adolescence,
it has strong religious overtones.

> Betet—betet für mich,
> Für meine arme Seele
> Ihr alten Frauen betet für mich,
> Für meine arme Seele. (*Vor dem Leben*, p. 163)

("Pray—pray for me, for my poor soul. You old women, pray for
me, for my poor soul.")
The poem paints a picture of a passive, helpless person, who must
depend wholly on others—in this instance, God—for survival. It is
at bottom the outlook of a child incapable of finding his own way
in the world and totally at the mercy of an unknown, unnamed parent, who has long since left the scene and abandoned Kaspar to his
own devices.

The second part, which forms the first of the remaining prose
passages, is entitled "Kaspar Hauser und die blinde Frau" (Kaspar
Hauser and the Blind Woman). Kaspar meets an old woman by the
roadside, who inquires about his origins and destination. He answers: " 'Oh—mother—I no longer know where I am to go.
—Once they told me the end of the journey, but I have forgotten
the word. And now I must find my way home without knowing the
way, for in these parts I will scarcely find a guide.' " (*Vor dem
Leben*, pp. 165-66) Totally uncertain about his destination, he expresses no doubts about where he came from: " 'I lived then in a
great palace—this palace stood by a lake. Over the lake fluttered
black birds. . . .' " (*Vor dem Leben,* p. 166) The woman recognizes something noble in his demeanor, for she addresses him as
"mein armer Prinz" (my poor prince), an appellation strongly
reminiscent of the other Kaspar in "Vor dem Leben I", where the
young prince follows an inner compulsion to leave his father's
house. We learn more about the present Kaspar's background
when he acknowledges: " 'I had a sister, too. . . . She always sang
the same song; the melody which my sister sang was always the
same.—But I have forgotten it.' " (*Vor dem Leben,* p. 167) The
old woman answers reassuringly: " 'You'll find the melody. You
have the longing for it, it will not let you go. Seek it, my poor
prince. . . . you will find it.' " (*Vor dem Leben*, pp. 167-68)

The remaining five vignettes follow a similar pattern of confrontation between Kaspar and a person whom he meets along the way. In almost every instance, the person he meets bears some affliction or is in some way, like himself, representative of society's outcasts. The second segment, "Kaspar Hauser und die reisende Hure" (Kaspar Hauser and the Travelling Whore), finds the hero in conversation with another of those unfortunates who tries to persuade him to stay with her because he has lost his mother: " 'You should travel with me, Kaspar Hauser . . . stay with me . . . Don't we have basically the same fate? Since you have lost your mother? Then we would both be helped.' " *(Vor dem Leben*, p. 171) In the preceding segment, it had been his sister's melody that was lost. Here it is his mother.

In "Kaspar Hauser und das irre kleine Mädchen" (Kasper Hauser and the Young Mad Girl), the relationship between the two protagonists is similar to the one in the preceding segment. An excited and disturbed young girl, who complains of being persecuted by her tyrannical father, mourns the loss of her mother, whom the father continues to torment even in death. Her anxiety about her father contains an indisputable hint of fear of sexual molestation: " 'He is so unprincipled—and how improper he is with me, I cannot even tell you.—At night he comes naked to me, when I want to sleep. He calls me 'little angel' and I am so afraid. So many men are good, but I have a bad father.'" (*Vor dem Leben,* p. 176) As the girl tries to lose herself in the woods, and Kaspar pursues her in an attempt to help her, he is suddenly struck by a new thought: "Still, it seemed to him, as he saw her dancing, that it must be possible for him, nonetheless, to help the tormentedly hopping one. Because there was, as he thoughtfully comprehended, nearly a brother-sister bond between them, more than he had at first thought—because she was only his little wayward sister." (*Vor dem Leben*, p. 178) He seems to have found the sister whom he had earlier lost. There is a hint of predestination here, a suggestion that these two were fated to meet and that he was destined to help her. But as he continues to pursue her, and she, in turn, continues to evade him, still another thought enters his mind: "And, as so often before, Kaspar thought, running through a dark forest behind a strange, demented child, 'Perhaps—she—will help—me.—' " (*Vor dem Leben*, p. 179) The thought that he might be as dependent on her as she is on him is a strange and rather disturbing one. At this point the girl loses herself in the woods for the last time; and Kaspar, depressed about not being able to find her, returns to his carriage, prepared to continue his fruitless journey.

In the next episode, "Kaspar Hausers Freund" (Kaspar Hauser's Friend), Kaspar continues his journey and comes upon the corpse of a young man lying by the wayside. The corpse, evidently that of a man in his late twenties, is in the first stages of decay; but it is apparent from his more salient features that he is very handsome: "His head slightly askew, a strange smile on his features, which he himself would not have been able to interpret, Kaspar, kneeling, looked down on the motionless and slender yellowed hands of the corpse, which had been arranged, artificially and highly decoratively, on the black silk cloth of the jacket. So beautiful, thought Kaspar, and his face became more and more tender, the hands of the living are never so beautiful." (*Vor dem Leben*, pp. 181–82)

Apart from the apparent fascination with death which the story demonstrates, its homosexual implications are evident. But as the story continues, it becomes clear that it contains other elements which connect it thematically with previous segments of the Kaspar Hauser cycle. In his loneliness, Kaspar finds in the corpse temporary respite from his suffering, a friend whom he has been desperately seeking for so long. The corpse has the same meaning for him as the people whom he has encountered in previous episodes: he hopes it will provide him with the help and companionship which have eluded him thus far; it also provides him with a perverted form of sexual satisfaction. The morbid irony of the fact that the friend is dead merely adds to the futility of his entire quest: " 'But if we had found each other,' he said to him, 'don't you believe that everything would have been different—for both of us??'

"But the friend did not answer. And yet it was to Kaspar as if a great voice came to him and said: ' "And if it had then been otherwise," what kind of meaning and wisdom would that have had?' " (*Vor dem Leben*, p. 184)

If the story had been merely intended to display futility, it could easily have ended here, but the action around which its ending is constructed necessitates a deeper interpretation. As he becomes more and more infatuated with his dead comrade, it occurs to Kaspar, that he is able to visualize his friend's mother. As he does so, the mother appears from the bushes, wearing the headdress of a widow and smiling beatifically. At this moment, Kaspar is overcome with a tremendous feeling of relief and engages in a long and passionate kiss with the corpse. Beyond the obvious manifestations of homosexuality and necrophilia shown in these passages lies the figure of the mother, whose meaning for this episode is not immediately clear. References to a mother have been made in at least two of the previous episodes, and the wish for a sister which is partially fulfilled by the temporary appearance of the wayward little girl has been expressed. Here, the mother performs a kind of redemptive function because, as she smiles benevolently over the concluding scene, she grants legitimacy to the homosexual nature of the relationship.

A note of tenuous optimism in the otherwise morbidly fatalistic scenario of the *Kaspar Hauser Legenden* is injected into the next-to-the-last, and shortest, of the episodes, entitled "Kaspar Hausers Traum von Morgen" (Kaspar Hauser's Dream of Tomorrow). Kaspar has a dream in which he is surrounded by a group of blond-haired nubile youths who lavish all manner of exotic fruits on him, which they carry in baskets. These are joined by a group of horses, rearing and whinnying as they "pranced joyously around Kaspar Hauser, the child of the evening and of the great darkness, celebrated him, the sickest child of this world, as lord and hero of their power." (*Vor dem Leben,* p. 189) As in the preceding episode, the homosexual aspect is evident. What makes this episode significant, however, is the sense of orgiastic celebration of a personality who is, according to all realistic criteria, worthy of nothing but the profoundest pity. It is representative of a certain kind of self-deluding optimism which will be seen to exist in the final episodes of a number of Klaus Mann's early works and which will prove to be of relevance to his work in general.

The final chapter, "Der tote Kaspar Hauser" (The Dead Kaspar Hauser), possesses the same fairy-tale mood and imagery as the preceding one. Kaspar's funeral cortege is accompanied by six youths and seven women, whose presence is consistent with the symbolic structure of the previous episodes. Both represent collective forms of the dominant symbolic figures in the key episode, "Kaspar Hausers Freund." The youths are his friends, and they celebrate his death with laughter and in high spirits. The women are a collective representation of the mother figure, and they mourn his death with weeping: "So the seven women wept over their dear son. So the six youths laughed about their dear, dear friend. This caused no end of astonishment among those who had not known who Kaspar Hauser was." (*Vor dem Leben,* p. 192) Even within the description of death, the fundamental ambivalence continues to operate. Death is greeted with a mixture of joy and grief, mourning and rejoicing. One is led to believe that the author is playing with the notion of death, as in the earlier episode, where it is treated with a similar mixture of affect. The association of death with homosexuality, as in "Kaspar Hausers Freund," which depicts the hero making love to a corpse, is a manifestation of a similar underlying motivation. All such contradictions are resolved, however, as an image of Christianity, which will appear at similar climactic junctures in his later work, dominates the final scene: "What was it, however, that brought the multitudes to their knees, as if the bishop were carrying the body of the Lord past them. And what compelled them to fold their hands and to lower their faces in deep joy as in deep pain, as if the Son of Man were tarrying in their wretched midst?" (*Vor dem Leben*, p. 194)

The cornerstone of Klaus Mann's "Kaspar-Hauser-complex," the figure of Kaspar as a wandering, childlike, helpless character who embodies both conscious and unconscious autobiographical attributes, finds its first highly articulated expression in the *Kaspar Hauser Legenden*. It remains to be determined if similar features exist in subsequent works, and, if so, to what extent changes in the author's style and outlook might have produced variations and offshoots of this basic theme.

II   Anja und Esther

Anja und Esther, Klaus Mann's first published play, was written in 1925. Classified "A Romantic Play," it takes place in a "convalescent home for fallen children," which is deliberately and satirically modelled after the *Odenwaldschule*, with the character of *Der Alte* (The Old One), its benevolent but somewhat distracted director, being an undiguised parody of Paul Geheeb. The play concerns the loves and intrigues of four of the school's long-standing wards, Anja, Esther, Kaspar and Jakob, whose already precarious relations are disturbed by the sudden appearance of Erik, a handsome, worldly outsider. It becomes evident that Erik is the key figure in the plot because his relationship with Esther is the catalyst in the dissolution of all the other relationships:

For Erik was wildly attractive, the veritable incarnation of sex appeal. A sailor, an adventurer, an enthralling brute, he invades the conventual (sic) dance academy. With his sweeping appetite for love, food, and fun, he bewitches and upsets the bittersweet idyll of Anja and Esther and the anemic kids. The emotional relations among the members of the little group become perturbingly complicated.[4]

Erik is a disruptive influence in the cloistered life of the school, not because he deliberately sets out to disturb the emotional equilbrium of the principal characters, but because their existence is a contrived, artificial one to begin with, and his presence represents the shocking influence of the "real" world, which is preparing to dissolve their dream-like *modus vivendi*. Erik's affair with Esther—the maturest and the most responsible of the group—culminates in her decision to leave the school. This decision leaves Anja depressed, Kaspar confused, and it launches Jakob into a homicidal mood.

The occasionally comic mood of the play, along with its homosexual overtones, does not, however, mask its serious philosophical content. As in most of Klaus Mann's writings of this period, the situation of adolescents in crisis, the emotional and psychological conflicts which exist in a group of young people who unhappily find themselves in the state of being "before life" is clearly, if at times surrealistically, depicted.

III   Die Jungen

A thematic precursor to *Anja und Esther* can be found in *Die Jungen* (The Youths), the first story in the volume, *Vor dem Leben*. It was written at the age of sixteen, shortly after Klaus left the *Bergschule Hochwaldhausen*, where his own adolescent experiences provided him with the mood and background for the story. As in *Anja und Esther*, the primary motivation for the plot is the decision of one of the main characters, Maria, to leave the school. The school is headed by an ultra-liberal professor—though not as benevolent as "The Old One"—who founded it according to a radical *laissez-faire* philosophy, designed to enable the students to educate themselves with a minimum of discipline imposed from above. Through relatively minor but repeated violations of this code of behavior, Maria has fallen out of favor with her superiors and must be routinely punished. As a consequence of these infractions and punishment and the unrest which had been building in her for a long time, she decides to leave. The other students, whose disaffection with the school and its director parallel hers, give her aid and encouragement in her resolve.

The mood of disillusionment and rebellion which pervades the school is similar to that which existed among the students during Klaus Mann's brief tenure at *Hochwaldhausen* and which he undoubtedly shared with them: "In the *Jungen* is contained that which signified the basic mood of our existence at that time: the destructive, negating passion—this passion growing out of a strong vitality, which is, however, still so uncertain about its own goals and possibilities that there exists no other release for its expression than that of melancholy and the bitter joy of self abasement." (*Kind*, p. 171) Combined with the general feeling of discontent and mischief which one would expect to find among adolescents in a boarding-school is a deeper and more disturbing spirit of nihilism and despair, which is also the primary undercurrent in *Anja und Esther*. On more than one occasion, the students express thoughts of death or suicide. Harald, Maria's friend and confidant, who bears the closest resemblance to Klaus Mann himself, remarks on the occasion of Maria's departure: " 'Yes, now she will probably soon die.' " (*Vor dem Leben*, p. 32) This apparent *non sequitur* and Harald's presentation of it in such a way as to attempt to hide the thought from those present has a startling effect on the reader. On another occasion, he makes a remark which is an accurate intimation of the author's own sentiment at the time the work was written: " 'The world is wide—I will go into a cabaret, I will play in the theater, I will write poems—life is not boring, especially since death always stands at the end of it.' " (*Vor dem Leben*, p. 44) Toward the end of *Anja und Esther*, Anja comments to Kaspar: " 'In any case, it seems to me as if youth had never concerned itself so much and so fervently with death. We don't often talk about it. But in everything we do, there is the thought of it.' " (*Anja und Esther*, p. 42)

Conflict between the generations, which is strongly evident in the relationship between students and teachers in *Die Jungen*, and which threatens to destroy the very existence of the school, is also present, although less manifestly so, in *Anja und Esther*. The utopian and, at the same time, authoritarian posture of the professor in the former—traits which are evidently self-contradictory—becomes tempered in the benevolent and omniscient figure of "The Old One." Klaus had a tolerance and respect for Paul Geheeb which he did not have for his professor at *Hochwaldhausen*:

The principles of our professor and leader seemed to be the most modern of all, although he himself was not of a radical, but rather of a bourgeois-moderate nature. . . . Progressive, kind, and intelligent enough to permit us great freedom, he lacked the personal power of suggestion and the psychological sensitivity to deal with the blossoms which our dangerous and beautiful freedom nourished so eccentrically. (*Kind*, p. 166)

And, in contrast:

He was of a great tolerance and magnanimity, he seemed to observe and tolerate much, without lifting a finger. But somehow it was always *he* who held all the reins—in great contrast to the professor of the *Bergschule,* who made such an honest effort. Geheeb's pedagogical personality hardly had to interfere with the day-to-day activities of the school; it had an effect because the consciousness of its existence remained apparent—more or less clearly—to everyone. (*Kind,* p. 182)

In addition to the tension between the students and their professor which becomes clearly evident as the story of *Die Jungen* unfolds, there are also indications of a conflict between the main characters and their parents in both *Die Jungen* and *Anja und Esther,* the existence of which, as we have seen, Klaus Mann was loath to acknowledge as far as his own life was concerned. Numerous characters in both works, however, are preoccupied with questions about their respective parents' attitudes toward them. Esther, whose father is a renegade Catholic priest, is highly critical of his treatment of her: "'My father had once been a Catholic cleric, but he left the confines of the Church in scandal. Still, he always went around in a frock-coat and tormented us as though he were the Grand Inquisitor.'" (*Anja und Esther,* p. 33) Anja, whose father is a high-ranking military officer, complains that he all but abandoned her: "Even when she [Anja] speaks of this father, who today would not hesitate for a second simply to disown her as his daughter, there is something like sympathy in her voice." (*Anja und Esther,* p. 33) Harald, whose father is also an officer, is perturbed by his father's lack of esteem for him. His friend Adolf, upon hearing of Harald's intentions to join the theater and write poetry remarks: "'Your father would call that slovenly.'" (*Vor dem Leben,* p. 44) Sentiments of this nature are probably similar to those which young Klaus had had with regard to his fathers's attitude toward his own artistic ambitions. Although it is unlikely that Thomas Mann would have considered his son's decision to become a writer "slovenly," it is well known that he and his family were skeptical about his intention and tried to dissuade him from it.[5]

What becomes most apparent to the reader after he takes both works into consideration is the exaggerated mood of sensuality and the precocity, both intellectual and sexual, of the main characters. Although both works are ostensibly about young adolescents — Erik, one of the oldest, is only eighteen, and the characters in *Die Jungen* are presumably considerably younger — their outward demeanor and characteristics of speech are those of adults. Although they are riddled with doubts about their futures and are unsure of their own aspirations, they express themselves with the eloquence and self-assurance of the maturest adults. Such bold demeanor is reflected in their haughty repudiation of their superiors' attempts to discipline them: " 'I do not know,' said Adolf and carried his head straight as a candle, 'whether Doctor Fehr or whether you, my esteemed Professor, are capable of comprehending to what essentially insignificant symptoms, like this so-called lack of discipline, can be reduced.'" (*Vor dem Leben,* p. 15) In contrast, the real adults in the story are given to displays of inappropriate emotion and behave, in many instances, like children. Dr. Fehr, one of the two adults, suffers both from a psychological inability to complete a book he has been trying to write and from a frustrated love affair with one of the students, Sybille. The end of the story finds him a helpless incompetent, crying bitterly over his failures. The professor, meanwhile, is pictured as a blustering tyrant who continues to cherish his hopelessly far-fetched pedagogical ideals.

It seems evident that, in these early works, Klaus Mann was attempting to convey a satirical impression of life in the kind of boarding school environment he experienced as a youth. On a deeper level, however, he also gives an incisive, if somewhat stylized description of the pain and confusion which are part and parcel of every adolescent's attempt to dissolve and strictures of parental authority on the way to becoming an autonomous adult. It is most probable that these early writings also express and alleviate some of the pain and confusion which Klaus Mann experienced as part of a similar process.

IV   Der fromme Tanz

In 1925, not long after the publication of *Vor dem Leben*, Klaus Mann wrote *Der fromme Tanz* (The Devout Dance), his first full-length novel. It was his first opportunity for extended character treatment and plot development. The setting of the novel, chiefly Berlin and Paris, and numerous characters and events are once again drawn directly from the author's personal experience. Its hero, Andreas Magnus, possesses many attributes of Klaus Mann's personality.

The son of a well-to-do and successful father—the mother is, in this case, dead—Andreas suddenly feels compelled to leave his family, not because they have wronged him in any way, or are encouraging him to leave, but because he feels a strong, yet indefinable, sense of malaise at the prospect of remaining with them. Early in the novel, he describes a kind of subdued adolescent crisis, similar to that which Klaus himself had experienced and which he had earlier described in the story "Vor dem Leben I". The situation with which Andreas must come to grips is described early in the novel:

He was not to blame, and his father was not to blame. No one was to blame. But everything had been that way.—His father had certainly wanted to help and had said: "You see, my son, we have all gone through that at one time—that is puberty—those are the perils of youth—." And then the son had cast down his eyes and had not answered or said anything to the effect that it was something else, not the psychic-physical crisis of the transitional years, but rather a peril, a rift of a deeper, more trenchant, more fateful kind. (*Fromme Tanz*, pp. 29-30)

The adolescent crisis in which Andreas finds himself can only be resolved by yielding to the urge to move, to go out into the world and confront both its promises and perils. Andreas is a young man with a conscience, who struggles with antithetical desires, which he is only partially able to reconcile:

So he strolls about—floating, forlorn, hazardously uprooted; an intellectual vagabond and ecstatic tramp. He is childish and sophisticated, genuine but coquettish, saturnine, but reckless, lascivious but without guile. Always in a haze of melancholy, in a delirium of loneliness, he keeps exploring, insatiably, the sordid little secrets of the underworld, the great treasures of world literature, and the landscapes of human faces. He is disorganized and wasteful: rich in imagination, poor in discipline. (*Turning Point*, p. 114)

Niels, the other protagonist, is a one-dimensional character. Entirely without remorse, untroubled by pangs of conscience or even second thoughts, he manoeuvers carelessly from one relationship to another. He is the complete gigolo, living from the wealth of older women, and leaving them when they no longer satisfy his needs, or when a more propitious opportunity comes along. He is also bisexual, in contrast to Andreas, who is exclusively homosexual.

The relationship which develops between Andreas and Niels follows a similar pattern of love and hate, in which Niels continues to play the same role as with his other lovers, and Andreas is constantly forced to bear the pain of his rejection. The relationship is complicated by the role of Franziska, who has a strong albeit Platonic, attachment to Andreas, but who succumbs dramatically to the advances of Niels, while Andreas is forced into the humiliating position of a helpless onlooker. Afterwards, Niels apologizes superciliously, but it is evident that considerable damage has already been done to Andreas's self-esteem. Nevertheless, Andreas continues to keep the company of both Niels and Franziska.

Shortly after this scene, there is a section of the novel which is of special significance both because it represents a climax in the story, and because the narration suddenly becomes symbolic:

Dear Niels, I almost believe I know everything about us. We are two children who have lost their way in the forest and cannot find each other. The one child has many thoughts in his head and much doubt—but the other has sort of blonde hair. . . . I call your name, you are called Ugolino. "Ugolino!" I cry into the air. Perhaps you are also calling my name somewhere, I hear your cooing voice from a distance. My name is Kaspar.—But our names do not find each other, the wind plays games with their syllables, it throws them around so, they meet—oh, they cross in the black air. Kaspar cannot see you, Ugolino, you are strange, lost, irretrievable between the bushes—sometimes you stand still, are suddenly quiet like a tree, but he fails to recognize you for the second time—your tree-like silence is not like your restlessness—and he runs past you once more. (*Fromme Tanz*, pp. 183-84)

The name Kaspar, linked to the image of the wandering, homeless youth, occurs once more in Klaus Mann's work. The passage described is almost identical with the scene in *Kaspar Hauser und das irre kleine Mädchen* in which Kaspar pursues the little girl and finally loses her in the forest. The name Ugolino, undoubtedly a reference to a character originally created by Dante and to the title character of Gerstenberg's *Sturm und Drang* drama, requires some interpretation. The context clearly indicates that Niels and Andreas are to be compared to two lost children, trying in vain to find each other in the forest. It is also clear that Niels is deliberately trying to evade Andreas. The name Ugolino, referring to the father who is forced to starve to death in a dungeon with his two children, implies that both Niels and Andreas are "starving" in an emotionally barren environment, the one searching for a fulfillment which the other can never provide.

Despite the futility of their relationship, Andreas continues to seek contact with Niels, who in turn continues to try to avoid him. Andreas pursues Niels to Paris, where he has been living with a Scandinavian sculptress. Finally, convinced that Niels will never change and that the promise of any lasting relationship between them is destined never to be fulfilled, Andreas resolves once again to seek his fortune in an unknown, but slightly less hostile world.

Before coming to this seemingly abrupt decision, Andreas is moved to write a letter to his fiancée, Ursula Bischof, whom he has not seen since he made the decision to leave his home and family. At crucial moments in the story, as in the scene of Niels's infidelity just described, Andreas is prompted to recall events relating to his former life. He implies that he will one day return to Ursula, but that he must, for the moment at least, continue to travel, to wander in quest of continued sensual fulfillment: "All trees rustle for me, all seas wait for me. Men sit in their living rooms, whom I have to meet next. The human body is beautiful in all its parts. I love the human body." (*Fromme Tanz*, p. 294)

The apparent optimism of the ending obscures the fact that the novel could just as easily have ended badly for the main character. The evident light-heartedness and *Lebensfreude* of the hero mask a potentially tragic undercurrent which exists from the very beginning of the novel. Andreas's friend and colleague, Paulchen, commits suicide in pursuit of Andreas; it is not difficult to imagine Andreas doing the same as a consequence of a final attempt by

Niels to spurn him. Instead, Andreas turns a potentially tragic situation into one which appears, for the moment, stable. But even with all the varied experiences and emotional entanglements to which the hero is party, he achieves little true gain or genuine personality development in the end.

One character in the novel who possesses some measure of stability is Franziska. With the exception of her single indiscretion with Niels, she remains loyal to Andreas, and even though she recognizes the impossibility of being his lover, she presents herself as a true friend, displaying kindness and understanding. When she learns that she is pregnant by Niels, she accepts her difficult situation with quiet optimism. Here, the birth of a baby represents a ray of hope, the promise of a new beginning, in what would otherwise have been a dreary, purposeless existence.

As Andreas is about to make his fateful decision to leave Niels forever, he once again sinks into a dream-like state which signals the onset of climactic changes throughout the novel. He is visited by angels:

There at first he heard the beating of angels' wings. He could not open his eyes, and thus he could not see the angels. But he felt their presence, their silvery noises made with wings and instruments, their holy-soundless speech. They crowded around him, the whole room was already filled with them. They must have stepped out of the walls, the entire hotel room was full of angels, pressing hard; they surrounded the tired one in his wide bed. (*Fromme Tanz*, pp. 290-91)

From the midst of the angels appears a regally dressed female figure, who had appeared in a similar dream scene at the very beginning of the novel. There, the figure had represented the mother of God, and Andreas had offered her a wreath of roses, which she had refused with the admonition: "Before I deign to accept your homage you must have experienced greatness." (*Fromme Tanz*, p.21) When the apparition appears once again in the final scene, this time it is he who refuses to give her a wreath, with the explanation that he has already placed it around a picture of Niels, thus dedicating his love and allegiance to another, who is both mortal and male.

The scene bears striking similarity to the the final scene of *Kaspar Hausers Freund*, where a mother figure appears and gives a kind of blessing to a relationship which cannot exist. Here, the mother figure is extended into the symbolic counterpart of Catholicism and also ties the end of the novel to its beginning, providing the entire work with a sense of thematic unity. Andreas is charged with a mission which he must complete in order to reach a predetermined goal. His final decision to dedicate the wreath to Niels rather than to a religious symbol represents a partial repudiation of that goal. The decision can, on the one hand, be considered as a continuing declaration of homosexuality, since Niels was his lover; but on the other hand—undoubtedly what Klaus Mann consciously intended—it can be seen as a rejection of otherworldly and basically negative ideals in favor of an affirmation of life, a kind of Faustian urge to experience all of life's potential, without regard for the consequences:

He is lonely because he seeks freedom, nothing but freedom, extreme independence. He jeopardizes all his privileges, betrays his responsibilities: for what? For a dazzling chimera called Life, life as such; as unending movement, sensual spell, meaningless miracle. He thinks he is strong enough to get away with his risky ecstasies without any guide or goal; without security, home, or lasting human relations; advised by nobody and nothing except his own impulses and visions, completely isolated and completely free. (*Turning Point*, pp. 114-15)

That a person can be completely isolated and, at the same time, completely free seems to be a contradiction in terms. Whether Andreas has attained the goal of true fulfillment is doubtful; what is striking about his function in the novel as a whole is how closely his situation resembles that of Klaus Mann at the time the work was written: "By no means is he lighthearted or frivolous. The thought of death is powerful in his mind, although he summarizes his credo in the words: I believe in this life. But the life he means is a sacred adventure, a devout dance.

"He is very young." (*Turning Point*, p. 115)

V Kindernovelle

Kindernovelle (Children's Novella), written in 1925 as well, is a shorter work which also contains a number of distinctive autobiographical details. The most apparent ones are derived from the author's childhood. The children of the story and the setting in which they live present some striking correspondences to Klaus Mann's early life. There are four children in the story, Renate, Heiner, Fridolin and Lieschen. Renate is nine; Heiner, eight; Fridolin, seven; and Lieschen, five. They correspond in sex and approximate age to the four eldest Mann children at the time the Mann family spent their summers in Bad Tölz, in Upper Bavaria. The Manns occupied a house there during the years 1909 to 1918, when Klaus was between the ages of three and twelve. The youngest Mann Children, Michael and Elisabeth, had not yet been born.

Some elements from Klaus's own life were inserted directly into the plot without any attempt to disguise their origins. The games which Klaus and Erika played as children, as well as the elements of the secret language which they developed are daily fare for the children in the story. A teacher named Burkhardt, which is the name of a tutor whom the Manns hired for the children in Bad Tölz, and a section in which the children view the dead body of a baker's apprentice, which is described in some detail in the first chapter of *Kind dieser Zeit*, were also derived from the author's experience. The eldest boy, Heiner, who has the greatest penchant for creativity, bears the strongest resemblance to Klaus himself. He writes a poem which is very similar, both in meter and subject matter, to *Der böse Mörder Gulehuh* and the other sadistic poems which Erika and Klaus composed at an early age:

> Der stolze Jüngling Sündebab
> Verlor am Montag seine Hab':
> Drob schrie und jammerte er sehr,
> Das war ja fürchterlich und mehr. . . . (*Kindernovelle*, p. 21)

("The proud youth Sündebab lost his worldly goods on Monday: Thereupon he cried and lamented much; that was indeed terrible, and more. . . .")

Other autobiographical features in the novella are, first, the figure of the mother, Christiane, behind whom the character of Katja Mann is readily discernible. Second, although the father in the story is absent, his former presence is attested to by a death-mask, which perpetually hangs over Christiane's bed as a constant reminder of the influence he exerted on her. Like Thomas Mann, he had been a distinguished and somewhat controversial writer, whose works were well-known all over Europe. Unlike Thomas Mann, however, he was a former Catholic priest who had undergone a sudden conversion and had begun polemicizing against the Church. In this respect he is almost identical with Esther's father in *Anja und Esther*, who is known only by the fact that he is a renegade priest.

With the appearance of the main character, Till, and along with it the advent of the principal action of the story, the most palpable autobiographical elements cease. Yet even Till, who is but one representative of a type of character which appears in almost all of Klaus Mann's narrative prose works, was consciously derived, at least in part, from the young French writer René Crevel, one of his intimate acquaintances:

But when I met him [Crevel], he still was eager to live, to accomplish something, to play, to love, to fight, and to create. Indeed, he was dynamic enough to conquer my drowsy belle, the motherly ingenue surrounded by four healthy kids, awaiting the seducer. The character I had been seeking so long for my story—there he was: incalculable, dashing, lovable and complex. . . . He seems winged by extra-mundane powers — puerile, iridescent, chivalrous — as he invades the bedroom of the nostalgic widow: "Me voila! I am the most experienced yet most naive creature on earth — a young European intellectual." (*Turning Point*, p. 122)

Like those of his predecessors, Kaspar Hauser, Erik, and Niels, Till's origins as well as his future are obscure. He is twenty-one years old, a writer who seems to have had little success in his creative endeavors, and whose only living relative is a brother who lies critically ill in a hospital, awaiting death. Like so many of Klaus Mann's creations, he is a wanderer, eternally on the move, without a home, without lasting friendhips. Yet with all his apparent isolation he does not at first give the impression of being lonely or unhappy. He projects a kind of devil-may-care attitude toward life, which remains consistent through much of the novella. He seems to have boundless faith in his intellectual abilities, although little evidence of them is ever manifested. The books and papers he possesses indicate a wide range of interests, many of which border on the radical and esoteric: "Such a hodgepodge of periodicals, brochures and books she [Christiane] had never seen before. Next to the Beriner Illustrierte [Nietzsche's] *Will to Power,* the New Testament next to an American fashion magazine, a paper on sexual pathology next to Buddha's speeches, scientific works next to questionable Parisian novels, mixed in with brochures about Russia, many photographs, Cubist drawings, dolls." (*Kindernovelle,* pp. 48-49) As the children, who develop an increasing fondness and admiration for their new-found friend, express wonder over the variety of his memorabilia, he replies with a self-satisfied smile: "Yes, yes, I am a young European intellectual!" (*Kindernovelle,* p. 49)

As the story continues, Till develops an increasingly close relationship with the children, especially Heiner, the oldest boy. They spend many hours together, walking in the woods, while Till tells them fantastic stories about the origin and nature of man.

The central theme of the novella, however, concerns the deepening relationship between Till and Christiane and its startling resolution. Till's original motivation for meeting Christiane was his admiration for her late husband and his desire to learn something from his great work. The erotic attachment which develops between them is, typically, fostered and encouraged by her, with only a gradual and passive acquiescence on his part. In short, she seduces him. Relationships of this kind occur in several of Klaus Mann's early works. One of the most provocative is described in the short story *Der Vater lacht* (The Father Laughs) in the volume *Vor dem Leben,* where incest is prompted by a daughter's seduction of her father. In the story *Sonja,* appearing in the same collection, the heroine, a typically lonely and sexually frustrated girl, lives out her life in bucolic isolation until a pair of young drifters comes to her cottage. She quickly forms an attachment to the older and, with very few preliminaries, they make love. The boy never says a word, while her impassioned comments in anticipation of the love-making are, "Thank you—thank you—thank you." (*Vor dem Leben,* p. 105) Niels, in *Der fromme Tanz,* displays a similar pattern of behavior in his relationship with the wife of a privy councillor, with whom he becomes involved in one of his frequent excursions. In all these instances, the sexual activity is perfunctory, shallow, and bereft of deeper meaning. It is characteristic of the kind of activity which accompanies an adolescent's first sexual encounters; even the adverse feelings of guilt and self-reproach which can be part of a serious sexual relationship are lacking here.

From Christiane's point of view, her relationship with Till takes on a deeper meaning. It is clear that she is attached to him from the very beginning, although it appears that her initial reaction is one of infatuation with his youthful charm and carefree lifestyle. It is only after he continues to seek her company and the children's—he has apparently long since lost interest in her late husband's work—that the strength of her attraction to him increases: "She desired him more from day to day, the less she could follow his restless conversations. When he played in the garden with her children, she stood by the window and looked only at him. She loved each of his movements." (*Kindernovelle*, p. 58)

The deepening relationship between them demands its price, however. Between his moods of apparent lightheartedness and joy, Till is subject to fits of dark depression: " 'Why must those who are condemned to life do penance? It is a sickness, an abominable curse—' And then suddenly, breaking out in a childlike and primitive lament: 'I would so like to die—I would so like to be dead—I am so disgusted—.' " (*Kindernovelle*, p. 60)

While Till becomes more morose, Christiane grows firmer in her resolve to have him as her lover. Far from showing evidence of being desperately in love with him, her passion is dominated by a single overriding motive, the wish to bear another child. After their one night of lovemaking, Christiane blissfully pauses to reflect over the recent events, and, as if by sudden inspiration, an awareness comes over her: " 'There are two kinds of life,' she thought slowly, 'The resting and the moving. There are two kinds of longing: that which drives further and that which accepts. When the resting and the moving life have a wedding: That is conception.' " (*Kindernovelle*, p. 68)

The next morning, suddenly and without explanation, Till declares that he is leaving. After some feeble attempts to dissuade him and a final futile request that he take her with him, Christiane accepts her ultimate fate with placid resignation. There follows the scene with the dead baker's apprentice, and the sight of death makes a strong impression on the children, Heiner in particular. Juxtaposed with this scene is a mock wedding ceremony performed by the children, in which Heiner and Renate are married. The symbolic relationship between the funeral and the wedding underscores one of the primary meanings of the story: that death and birth exist in a kind of continuum, and that when a life is taken, a new one is formed to replace it. When Heiner expresses anxiety over the death scene he has just witnessed, Christiane attempts to reassure him: " 'One can die any day,' he told Mama, confused and sobbing, 'each of us—perhaps there will be no more people left—'

"But Mama, sitting heavily in the chair by his side, answered quietly: 'But in place of those [who die] new ones are always born—' She bent over her crying son, and suddenly even her quiet face was wet with tears." (*Kindernovelle*, p. 91)

The birth of her new child, like that of Franziska in *Der fromme Tanz*, provides Christiane with a secret satisfaction, an element of new meaning in what would otherwise be a sterile existence. For Klaus Mann, here is an opportunity to express, using the fantasy world of children as a background, an instance where life wins out over death. The victory, however, is hard-fought and tenuous. In the final scene, as Christiane and the children benevolently view the newborn girl, the mother's comment reveals something of the pain with which the new creation was brought into the world; and its deliberate ambiguity indicates that she is not merely referring to the pain of childbirth: "She spoke down into the crib, very quietly as if she were betraying a secret: 'But this time I would have almost died.' " (*Kindernovelle*, p. 107)

VI Gegenüber von China

In 1929, shortly after the impromptu world tour which he and Erika jointly undertook, Klaus Mann wrote a play called *Gegenüber von China* (Across from China), which demonstrates some of the influences of his journey, particularly those stemming from his lengthy stay in the United States. It deals with the problems and conflicts arising among a group of students in a college in California when a worldly, intelligent European exchange student comes into their midst. The chief protagonist, Madeleine Selmanowitsch, is a young European of either French, German or Slavic origin—her exact nationality is deliberately kept ambiguous—who is initially welcomed into the circle of students, but whose inevitable emotional and erotic attraction to Ken, one of the group's most eligible males, leads to her being ostracized by the group and her eventual decision to leave America. On the surface, the play represents Klaus Mann's growing concern with the apparent incompatibility between a person whose primary interests are intellectual and one whose motivation is predominantly materialistic: "My concern was always to show the American as a personification of robust naiveté—full of strength, capable, of an almost striking lack of complexity—, while his transatlantic counterpart always appears as one who is sicklied o'er with the pale cast of thought, steeped in sorrow, initiated into various dark and questionable secrets." (*Wendepunkt*, pp. 204-05)

The Americans—with one exception—are accurately depicted according to the prevalent stereotype of the American college student: their primary interests are girls and expensive automobiles; their commitment to intellectual pursuits exists only to the extent necessary to pass their courses; they are cliquish and possessed of all the common prejudices of typical older middle-class adolescents. The girls, especially, remain true to this pattern. They belong to an exclusive sorority called the "Club of the Hard-boiled," which indulges in all manner of juvenile pranks and adolescent rituals. Billy, the president of the club and chief conspirator of the play, succeeds in ruining the career of a young athletic instructor, whom she had tried to seduce when she reports him to the authorities after he had refused to succumb to her advances. She is also chiefly responsible for Madeleine's resignation from the college by arranging for the members of the "Club of the Hard-boiled" to send a damaging letter about her to the school's directors. The real reason for this action is that Madeleine has managed to attract Robert, Billy's fiancé, away from her.

Madeleine is by far the maturest of all the characters in the play. Able to see through all the intrigues which are set up around her and disciplined enough to resist the advances of the boys who have become infatuated with her, she makes up her mind, with calm determination, to leave the college and go to China, where she has been offered an opportunity to work.

The one boy, and principal male character, who does not fall into the same stereotyped pattern as the others, is Robert. An intellectual and a musician, he rejects the frivolous activities of his companions in favor of more serious pursuits. Given to moods of melancholy, he, too, wishes to leave the vapid college atmosphere and go elsewhere, where the intellectual climate is more fulfilling. When Madeleine rejects his overtures as well, he contemplates suicide. His evaluation of his colleagues' ideas and goals is very pessimistic:

These empty faces, etched by no thought, no adventure? These brows, blank and silly and dumb from a stultifying optimism, which finds our time the most magnificent imaginable of all times, because it simply confuses the most mundane fight for the dollar and material goods with freedom. One looks just like the other, and they all want to be in thirty years what their mothers and fathers are today. (*Gegenüber von China,* pp. 54-55)

He draws a comparison between Europe and America:

I think Europe has shown us what youth means: effort, idealism, struggle for a spiritual goal. Who cares about the spirit, here, in the most famous universities of this magnificent land? I do not know *one* young man between these walls whose ambition is directed toward anything other than being practically, purposefully equipped for the economic struggle for survival. (*Gegenüber von China*, p. 55)

Although this picture of American—in contrast to European —youth as a group of dull-witted materialists is an oversimplification, it is a reflection of a problem which was to concern Klaus Mann, increasingly and in more sophisticated terms, for the remainder of his life: the role of the intellectual in shaping the world around him.

Between 1925 and 1930, Klaus Mann wrote a series of essays in which he attempted to analyze the generation of which he himself was a member and to formulate a possible direction which contemporary youth might take in order to correct the errors of previous generations. In an essay entitled "Heute und Morgen," written in 1931, he characterized contemporary youth as being essentially at an impasse, in the midst of a moral and intellectual crisis in which they were becoming aware of the problems which their elders had been unable to solve, but were themselves unable to arrive at a solution. Youth itself was divided between those who clung to their intellectualism and those who became anti-intellectual and sought solutions to their conflict in radical political organizations: "Add to this the distrust of the intellect, which has become so strong by and by. From a malicious *hostility toward the intellect* to being fed up with the intellect, this distrust goes unmistakably through the entire generation. It is deeply rooted; we have certainly experienced an all too thorough renunciation of thought during all the years. This explains the enormous significance of sports, which prevails almost boundlessly in youth. It looks as though the events of this time have carried the intellect much too far *ad absurdum*."[6] The apparently irreconcilable conflict between the intellectual and the anti- or non-intellectual, which began to emerge as a theme in Klaus Mann's work at this time, inevitably invites comparison with Thomas Mann's *Tonio Kröger*, who became a symbol of a similar conflict in the previous generation. Yet Klaus Mann wanted to maintain a distinction between Tonio Kröger and the type of young intellectual which he envisioned:

The type which Tonio Kröger more or less symbolizes stands ironically, painfully, observing, knowing and outside. I see the other, *my* contemporary: perhaps not less knowing, perhaps even no less experienced in pain, but definitely no longer ironic. He stands otherwise bent over life, more carried away, blinder. He is less complicated, hence more innocent, but in a deeper sense. We have become more naive, beyond pain." (*Suche*, pp. 31-32)

Robert, who fits this pattern more closely than his predecessors, Till and Andreas, is, in many respects, Klaus Mann's counterpart to Tonio Kröger. While the latter is aware of his dilemma but is able to hold himself aloof from his blond-haired and blue-eyed contemporaries with an attitude of ironic detachment, the former finds himself in a more desperate situation, in which irony and detachment are no longer appropriate. While Tonio Kröger has respect, and even longs for the lifestyle which Hans Hansen represented, Robert has nothing but contempt for his colleagues, a sentiment which they, by and large, deserve. Even Madeleine, who, because of her position as an outsider to the group, can afford to be somewhat emotionally detached from them, ultimately finds herself in a position where she too can no longer tolerate their petty maliciousness.

Klaus Mann's "American" play offers a microcosm of the intellectual and emotional situation in which the author felt contemporary youth, in general, found itself. His portrayal of the antagonists in the play—which bears the subtitle "Comedy"—must not be construed as an indictment of American youth as such, but must rather be viewed as symbolic of that sector of youth with which Klaus Mann was most concerned, the European. While Madeleine represents all that is wholesome and encouraging within the European intelligentsia, the American college students represent all the petty, retrogressive, destructive tendencies of the European generation with which Klaus Mann was most closely associated. Since the latter was clearly uppermost in the author's mind when he was writing the play, and since it was involving itself more and more in the political affairs of Germany, the play assumes a distinctly political character.[7]

In an essay entitled "Wie wollen wir unsere Zukunft?" (How Do we Want our Future?), written in 1930, Klaus Mann further articulated his view of the crisis of youth by characterizing it as a universal phenomenon, which involves all generations and is only partially dependent on historical circumstances:

There have been two kinds of youth from the beginning: one which only lives, with more or less enthusiasm, more or less noise, glitter and élan; and one which at the same time *thinks*: that is, consciously shapes its life and has goals in mind, those for the day and hour, as well as more distant, utopian ones. The first group is by far the largest, and always has been; in addition, it is also the happier one. This is stated without envy; it is a fact. Thought destroys happiness. The joys which it affords are infrequent and problematical. (*Suche*, p. 92)

In outlining the basic dilemma of his time and in attempting to give some direction to those, including himself, who were involved in the struggle, he naturally turned his attention toward the political sphere, where much of the drama of which he and his generation were a part was being played out. Like most of his intellectual colleagues, he was very much disturbed by the regressive, reactionary tendencies of the non-intellectual majority, who were being lured in large numbers into the tantalizing illusion of what was to become National Socialism; but unlike many of them, he did not choose to espouse the ideology of Dialectical Materialism. Instead, he remained something of a political loner, an advocate of the utopian ideals of Ernst Bloch and the Pan-European movement of Count Coudenhove-Kalergi. His admiration for the latter's philosophy at times became unusually vehement: "Let us, above all, make our appeal with the simple instinct for survival, which is inherent in every organic life-form. *That it would be suicide to leave Europe disunited is a plain, irrefutable fact.* Let us make our appeal with life, which, along with reason, is on our side, against death, with which today all Nationalism is in league." (*Suche*, p. 91)

Although *Gegenüber von China* is not intended as a political play, it contains the rudiments of a conflict which could have evolved into a political one because the conflicting parties represent two opposing factions, two disparate life styles, which are incompatible in the long run. As Klaus Mann became more involved in the political ferment which was beginning to engulf his country toward the end of the 1920's, political motifs and themes began to appear with increasing frequency in his fiction; and the works which he published after 1930 contain, with very few exceptions, strong political components.

VII Adventures

In 1929, the same year in which *Gegenüber von China* was written, Klaus Mann published a collection of novellas called *Abenteuer*, in which overt political themes play a significant role. The first of these, *Abenteuer des Brautpaars* (Adventure of the Newlyweds), concerns a young couple, Gert and Jak, who meet by chance on a plane to Copenhagen, where Jak, a Communist, is scheduled to participate in a "Proletarian Youth Congress." Gert, a sculptress of American origin, has planned a rendezvous with her female lover. As in several previous works, the theme of homosexuality, plays a decisive role in the plot. During the flight, which is marred by a severe thunderstorm in which the plane and its passengers almost perish, Gert and Jak become sexually attracted to one another and decide to continue their relationship, which soon leads to their engagement.

Their relationship appears doomed from the start. Gert, in addition to being homosexual, is a freewheeling, irresponsible, childlike woman, who dashes heedlessly from one relationship to another in incessant and compulsive pursuit of pleasure. Upon her arrival in Copenhagen, she goes directly to the "Tivoli," where she spends the night going from one amusement to another and, in between, alternately attracting and rejecting a series of strange men. Jak, in contrast, is a dedicated Communist, whose excessive devotion to duty leads him into periods of melancholy and despair. In temperament and outlook, Gert could be considered a female counterpart to Niels, while Jak, with his moodiness and exaggerated sense of responsibility, bears closer resemblance to Andreas Magnus or Robert.

One would expect the instability of their relationship to end with a parting of the ways. Instead, there occurs an unusual development in both their situations which produces a modicum of hope that they might, after all, be able to establish a viable existence together. Jak suddenly becomes disaffected with Communism; and, after a dramatic confrontation with his comrade Georg, who accuses him of absconding with Party funds, he decides to leave the country. Gert, in turn, becomes sobered by his absence and begins to lead a more stable life. To complete this unexpected reversal in their attitudes, Jak begins a series of precarious adventures in Africa, where he is exposed to numerous unknown perils. Finally, Gert receives word that Jak is seriously ill in Tunis, and she resolves to make the journey to Africa so that she can be with him in his hour of need. The end of the story finds them reunited, but in a continued state of doubt and fear about their future together: " 'Georg has called us lost,' she whispered. He is right—oh, we have lost our grip. Don't you feel it?—That thing with the money, you know—that you still had to do that—it is only a sign, a symbol of our guilt—' " (*Abenteuer*, p. 76)

Despite the air of desperation surrounding their situation, Jak injects a note of optimism: " 'It begins with confusion. We begin with guilt. Because life is unfathomable. Georg does not need to understand anything about that. But don't you notice it? It is great. . . .' " (*Abenteuer*, p. 76) The mood of uncertainty tempered with hope is similar to that which Andreas Magnus experiences at the end of *Der fromme Tanz*. Although it would seem, from all outward appearances, that whatever gains these characters have made up to now are at best tenuous, the sense of mystery and adventure which life holds for them gives them encouragement to go on. Whereas, in the earlier work, life was characterized as a devout dance, in this one another term has been added to Klaus Mann's arsenal of symbols, that of adventure: "They lay on this dirty bed as if they were on a sailboat heading into a dangerous night; odors, masks, and adventures came at them out of the streaming darkness. They opened their eyes piously as they rode." (*Abenteuer*, pp. 76-77)

When one views the entire story in perspective, one notes that each of the main characters exhibits certain personality traits which are offset by opposite characteristics in the other. In the beginning, Gert, in her relentless pursuit of sensual pleasure, represents the infantile, irresponsible half of the pair, while Jak, with his zeal and political dogmatism, is Gert's polar opposite. In the latter half of the story, the polarity is reversed: Gert is suddenly stricken by pangs of conscience, while Jak totally abandons his previous austerity in favor of a life of adventure and high risk. One would expect that by the end of the story this dialectic would resolve itself in some way, and that in their final reunion the extremes of both personalities might become tempered into a stable synthesis. Such is not the case, however. Although they remain together at the end, the stability of their relationship and their prospects for future happiness, like those of Andreas Magnus, remain in doubt.

Although the political implications of this story are not an essential motivating factor in the plot, they provide a strong thematic undercurrent and continue to give some indication of the political concerns which Klaus Mann had at the time he was writing it. The instability of the main characters, while not directly motivated by political factors, is, like that of the protagonists of *Gegenüber von China*, partially symbolic of the unstable political situation in Europe. It is not coincidental that Jak, the zealous party-line Communist, is of Russian origin, nor that Gert, his frivolous, apolitical counterpart, is American: "Once he happened to say to her, 'Do you know, in the final analysis, we are not really compatible: you are an American, I am a Russian.' She answered cynically, 'I find it is not so bad. After all, we are both only rather degenerate Europeans.' " (*Abenteuer*, p. 46)

The second story in the volume, *Gegenüber von China*, which bears little resemblance to the play of the same name, is a comparatively lighthearted account of a young man's "adventures" in Hollywood, where he seeks his fortune as a movie actor. The climax of the story coincides with his decision to have his nose operated on in order to satisfy the whims of a fickle director. Despite contrary advice from friends, he goes ahead with the operation, justifying his decision with the rather gratuitous statement, "To suffer for the sake of an idea . . . is the prerogative of youth." (*Abenteuer*, p. 117) Even though the main character is basically an adolescent and, as such, is typical of the majority of characters in Klaus Mann's early works, the story's almost comic aspects render it by and large uncharacteristic of his writings up to this point, and it may best be classified among his more experimental creations. Suffice it to say, the end of the story leaves the hero unresolved in his quest for success and fame, but determined to continue in pursuit of adventures.

The third story, *The Life of Suzanne Cobière*, continues in the intense, serious vein of the first and even possesses some morbid characteristics. The heroine, Suzanne, is the product of a prominent Catholic family and a strict education. As in the case of other significant Klaus Mann characters, her father is a retired high-ranking army officer. Like Jak, Gert, and other characters in the book, she is prone to making hasty, impulsive decisions which dramatically alter the course of her life. The first of these is her decision to marry Dr. Mirois, which she makes quite suddenly on the eve of a planned world tour, over the objections of her parents.

Dr. Mirois is a learned man, an intellectual, the type of person with whom Suzanne has had little previous contact; and his erudition and intellectual curiosity are the primary reasons for her infatuation with him. Despite the fact that she adjusts quite well to her new, sophisticated life style, there is evidence of growing tension between them, particularly over the issue of his political philosophy, which contains vehemently nationalistic sentiments. When she expresses some contempt for his point of view, he retorts, "It is a question of the victory of civilization! . . . of the idea of democracy!" (*Abenteuer*, p. 133)

After his death on a battlefield in World War I, she continues to undergo a series of sudden and radical transformations, each of which marks a further deterioration of her character and ultimately leads her to a bizarre and tragic end. She adopts the living habits of a member of the Parisian counterculture, frequenting coffeehouses and art galleries and attending all manner of unconventional gatherings and costume parties. She becomes sexually promiscuous and obsessed with the relentless pursuit of pleasure and meaningless diversion: "She screams, she howls, seems torn to shreds by lust, burning with hysteria. She becomes comical in all her viciousness, carries on so very wildly and extravagantly as if she wanted to present a caricature of herself." (*Abenteuer*, p. 135)

The next change in her life occurs when she runs out of money and meets a benefactor, Mr. Collan, who offers her a job as a teacher in a small women's college in New York. She soon loses this job, along with a succession of others, and attempts suicide. Mr. Collan, who is instrumental in rescuing her, invites her to vacation with him in Tahiti. After she spurns his offer of marriage, she goes to Honolulu, where she organizes a native dancing troupe, which later becomes involved in her grotesque death.

The story exhibits numerous similarities to works previously discussed. The heroine's strict Catholic background, combined with her artistic temperament, gives her a strong resemblance to Andreas Magnus. Her compulsive need to experience pleasure is strongly reminiscent of Gert, and her fluctuations in mood and general discontent are characteristic of almost all major Klaus Mann characters encountered thus far.

The story does, however, contain one essential element which does not exist in previous works: In a typical early Klaus Mann work there is usually an air of strained optimism which leaves the characters in a state of apparent emotional stability, determined to press on in their endeavors. Although we have encountered occasional references to death and suicidal thoughts, *The Life of Suzanne Cobière* is the first published work by Klaus Mann (with the exception of the Kaspar Hauser cycle) in which a main character has, in fact, died. Suzanne's death, which is caused by a knife thrown by a spurned suitor during a brawl involving the dance troupe, is a bizarre, but at the same time logical conclusion to a life which has long been degenerating. The emotionally charged, almost orgiastic circumstances of her death provide a fitting correspondence to the manner in which she has conducted her life to that point. The "hysteria," which had become increasingly characteristic of her life, now becomes associated with her death. The final description of her corpse, in striking similarity to that of the dead Kaspar Hauser, amounts to a kind of beatification, a celebration of her death: "A miracle occurred, for silence set in like a thunderbolt. From a corpse with its folded hands there emanated such solemnity that the sailors, harbor whores, Negroes, and Chinese had to retreat into a timid semicircle.

"She lay on the podium with an inexorably severely prominent nose. Now, in death, she had regained the unapproachable gentility of her ancestors." (*Abenteuer*, pp. 162-63) The last paragraph is an ironic reminder that her life had been spent in defiance of all the ideals and values which her parental tradition represented, and that death was the only medium through which she could return to it.

VIII   Alexander

In 1930, Klaus Mann published *Alexander*, the first of three works of fiction to deal with a historical personality.[8] Here the author was less concerned with presenting the life of Alexander the

Great in historical detail than he was with depicting his main character in view of a certain artistic and ideological meaning which the personality of Alexander conveyed to him: "What intrigued me about my new hero was the almost outrageous insatiability of his dream, the enormous dimensions of his adventure. Since my world tour, I loved to think in planetary dimensions. The Macedonian wanted not only to conquer the world: For him it was a question of unifying it and making it happy under his scepter. Was it not the Golden Age, indeed, Paradise, which he wanted to bring about? What a childishly clever, what a divinely inspired utopia!" (*Wendepunkt*, p. 215)

If we wish to inquire into the author's motivation for writing such a book at this time, perhaps a few key words to take into consideration are "adventure," "childish," and "utopia." It is clear that Klaus Mann's work up to now had been overwhelmingly concerned with the depiction of characters who possess all the vigor of youth and can, at the same time, be considered adolescent: that is, they direct all their energies toward goals which they never clearly define, experiencing all the doubt, anxiety and turmoil attending such a conflict. Concurrently, we have seen similar characterizations of youth in Klaus Mann's essays and political writings, along with futuristic utterances about the role of youth in the formation of Pan-Europe and the new "utopian" society. Although *Alexander* is not, in the strictest sense, a political novel—and the author has made no apparent conscious attempt to link it to the European political situation of 1930—the character of Alexander remains a representation of two basic general attributes of adolescence: doubt and anxiety, which are the products of internal conflict, which is, in turn, partly sublimated into an insatiable urge to change the world and bring about utopia.

The seeds of the conflict which sprout into Alexander's lust for power and global recognition are sown early in his life. His mother, Olympias, a strong-willed woman who showers her son with an excess of affection while schooling him in the bloody, vindictive mythology of her people, provides the first major formative influences in the boy's character: "She revealed to her child, only to him, what she knew: it was the mystery of the bloody sacrifice and the resurrection in light." (*Alexander*, p. 15)

While Alexander forms a strong positive attachment to his mother during the years of his childhood, his relationship with his father becomes increasingly strained and reaches the breaking point when Philipp decides to abandon Olympias and, in the midst of vicious political intrigue, to take Kleopatra as his new wife. Although Alexander's hatred for his father reaches a peak at this juncture, there remains in him an undercurrent of respect and admiration for Philipp's prowess as a politician and warrior: "With an exactitude which came from hatred, Alexander observed, judged, tested the politics of his father. He came to the conclusion that he found them impeccable, but at the same time abhorrent." (*Alexander*, p. 37) This ambivalence of feeling about his father and the ideals which his father represented are destined to remain with him for the rest of his life. When Olympias informs him that he is not Philipp's son, his reaction is one of surprise and incredulity. He reacts similarly when told that she played a part in the plot to assassinate him.

With Philipp's death, the secret bond between mother and son is sealed. In a scene filled with emotion, Olympias reveals her ambitions for her son and her intention of occupying the throne as a result of his future conquests. She also prophesies that he will not live long: " 'You yourself will not live very long, my sweet son; I also do not know if you will ever be happy. But you are chosen to bring happiness to mankind, my Alexander! . . . You will force it into being with love and the sword! You will force it into being with your beauty, with your youth.' " (*Alexander*, p. 55) Alexander listens silently and resolutely as his mother delivers her solemn mandate.

In addition to his strong attachment to his mother, his close, life-long relationship to his two comrades-in-arms, Kleitos and Hephaistion, assumes a special significance in the novel. Both are depicted as close friends of Alexander from his early childhood, but in their relations to him they act as polar opposites. From the beginning, Hephaistion plays the role of a trusted friend, constant and loyal, and, at the same time, submissive in the face of Alexander's continued attempts to assert his dominance over him. Kleitos, on the other hand, while possessing the same basic loyalty to Alexander, is loath to acknowledge the latter's superiority and even assumes the role of rival, a fact which is a constant source of frustration for Alexander and eventually leads to Kleitos' death by Alexander's hand. When, during a festive gathering of Alexander's officers, Kleitos refuses to submit to his authority by praising him, Alexander slays him in a fit of jealous rage: " 'It is generally said that you have accomplished great deeds,' he heard the voice of Kleitos saying. 'I understand nothing of that. I have also not paid attention to it; I had other things to think about. In the world in which *I* live, Alexander, you have been able to change nothing. You have not even disturbed me. *I do not know you at all*,' he said slowly and looked at him with a merciless pensiveness." (*Alexander*, p. 149) Afterwards, in a mood of deep depression over the consequences of his impulsive act, Alexander asks Hephaistion to kill him, as a gesture of self-retribution. Hephaistion, of course, refuses. Alexander's guilt about his feelings toward his dead comrade is a manifestation of the same ambivalence which had existed in his feelings about his father. His violent refusal to submit to domination, in any form, by another man, is a cornerstone of his megalomania, a basic source of his suffering, but at the same time a prime motivating factor in his passion for conquest.

While Klaus Mann's conceptualization of Alexander's personality fully expresses the inner conflict which is a necessary precondition for the fulfillment of his hero's stated goals, special emphasis is also placed on his basic humanitarianism and his desire to improve the lot of the peoples he conquered. At the same time, however, Klaus does not overlook the tremendous sacrifice in human life which it took to achieve these goals, as well as the fact that the historical Alexander's main object of bringing peace and prosperity to his empire actually fell far short of realization.

Alexander's guilt and his basic ambivalence about his fundamental role in life are most imaginatively expressed in the last scene of the novel, in which Alexander, on his deathbed, confronts an angel. The angel, a deliberate anachronism, has been noted in connection with the final scene of *Der fromme Tanz* and is here given more detailed articulation as a representation of the hero's conscience, a means of passing judgment on his life. The scene takes the form of a confession, during which Alexander reviews significant events in his career and at the same time seeks the angel's opinion of them. When he brings up Kleitos, the angel's response is harsh: " 'You have sacrificed another, not yourself!' the angel admonished. 'You have failed significantly in your mission.' " (*Alexander*, p. 244) When, however, Alexander asks the essential question: " 'Will I then be able to set up the kingdom of happiness of earth?' ", the angel abruptly changes character and weeps.

After the angel's judgment is complete and Alexander confesses that he has failed in his mission to realize his utopian dream, the angel makes an unexpected revelation: " 'You will return, in another form.' " (*Alexander*, p. 246) Although the angel falls silent after Alexander's impassioned question: "*To set up the kingdom?*" there can be no doubt about its messianic implications. Andreas Magnus, as has been noted, is motivated by a similar sense of mission; and, like Alexander, who receives his mandate initially from his mother, he too is sent on his quest by a woman, the mother of God, who appears to him in a dream. In a similar hallucinatory scene with angels, Andreas abandons his original mission in favor of life, while Alexander, acknowledging his failure, dies, with the promise of one day returning to life in order to complete his unfinished task. Andreas fails to experience "greatness," but hopes to gain fulfillment in his life, while Alexander, whose real accomplishments are of unquestionable magnitude, dies with his greatest hopes unfulfilled. Whether or not he will one day return "in another form" remains an open question. With a mournful and adoring army looking on, he expires, making a gesture symbolic of the ambivalence which he was never able to resolve, even at the point of death: "With a forced smile, he apologetically raised his hand, which heretofore he had solely raised as a command." (*Alexander*, p. 247)

Klaus Mann's *Alexander* is a fictional representation of a historical subject. It follows with reasonable accuracy the known sequence of events in Alexander's life, and whatever liberties the author may have taken with the facts are meant to conform to a certain preconception of his hero's personality which he wished to express in artistic form. If he had wanted to limit himself exclusively to the facts, he would have written a biography, not a biographical novel. At the same time, it is no coincidence that the life and personality of the historical Alexander to some degree conform to a pattern similar to those of many of the characters in Klaus Mann's work thus far discussed. All are youthful, of approximately the age of Klaus himself at the time a given work was written, and all are in the throes of emotional conflicts which are normally found in adolescence and which bear at least superficial resemblance to those which Klaus was experiencing in his early efforts to become emotionally and artistically independent of parental influences. Numerous elements in the works relate directly to specific experiences which the author documents in other contexts, such as his life in

Berlin, his world tour, and his reminiscences of early childhood.

Of even more striking significance for the understanding of Klaus Mann's early work is a fairly constant element of instability in the personalities of the main characters which mirrors the impulsive behavior which Klaus himself exhibited during much of his adolescence. Andreas Magnus all but abandons a promising career as an artist and enters into a string of dubious relationships as a means of achieving a temporary sense of independence; Jak, the dedicated Communist, suddenly abandons his lofty ideals and begins a new life full of uncertainty and danger; Suzanne Cobiére renounces her bourgeois security in favor of a quasi-artistic career in which success becomes of vital, all-consuming importance. Almost without exception, the conflicts of the main characters are rarely resolved to the point where each is able to find a sense of permanence in his life. There is, to be sure, a hint of cautious optimism at the end of *Der fromme Tanz* and the novella, *Gegenüber von China*, where the main characters are determined to continue as before, in the hope that they will eventually find a better tomorrow. But even they, like most of the main characters in the other works, seem destined to live out their lives in a kind of emotional limbo, always in search of a fulfillment which seems forever to elude them. Some contemplate suicide as a means of finally solving their problems.

It would be reasonable to suppose that the predominance of adolescent themes in Klaus Mann's early work is a manifestation of the youthful author's adolescence and a reflection of the fact that he had not yet found any permanent solutions to his own problems—he was only twenty-four when *Alexander* was published. It would be equally reasonable to suppose that, as he grew older, the subject matter of his writings would become increasingly complex, and his characters would assume a degree of maturity proportional to his own maturity, intellectual as well as emotional. As his interest in political problems grew, along with an increasing sense of unease over the rapidly developing crisis in his own country, there emerged a natural avenue for further artistic expression in the form of politically-oriented fiction. The nature and scope of Klaus Mann's political activity and its concomitant representation in his fictional works will be treated in the next chapter.

CHAPTER 4

The Literature of Exile: 1932–39

I Treffpunkt im Unendlichen

TREFFPUNKT im Unendlichen (Meeting Point in Infinity) is Klaus Mann's next major published work after *Alexander* and his third novel. Although it was published in 1932, roughly a year before he was forced to renounce his German citizenship, it should not properly be included among his early works because it resembles, both thematically and structurally, his two major novels of exile, *Flucht in den Norden* and *Der Vulkan*, more closely than his significant prose works of the 1920's. Because it bears some resemblance to *Der fromme Tanz*, as will later be demonstrated, it would be best to classify it tentatively as a transitional work.

Although Klaus Mann was not yet forced to relinquish his residence in Germany, by the end of 1932 the insidious spirit of the Nazi movement had already become very evident; and the necessity for German intellectuals with a conscience to leave their country was becoming imminent: "The same feeling of anxiety and oppression can be found in the literary works [which date] from this period, the last ones, in fact which I was to complete and publish in Germany. It is not primarily my political polemics and notes which I am thinking of. They frequently have the forced, trusting, or unctuously rhetorical tone which is now embarrassing to me; more importantly, I am speaking of things in which my cares sought to express themselves in an artistic guise—that is to say a valid and genuine one. A novel and a play which I wrote at that time (1930-32) seemed to anticipate the pain of homelessness." (*Wendepunkt*, p. 262) Two main points should be noted: first, that the novel here alluded to, *Treffpunkt im Unendlichen*, contains some of the mood and the problems of works which Klaus was later to write in and about the exile;[1] and second, that it is partly an expression of his inner conflicts in artistic form. As has been noted, much of Klaus

Mann's work written up to this point contains references—some plainly evident, others in need of interpretation—to characters and incidents in his life, many of which coincide meaningfully with the time at which a given work was written. If the novel presently under discussion remains true to this pattern, an assumption which the author's statement supports, we should expect to find numerous autobiographical references woven into its fabric, some of which may be essential to its basic structure.

The two main characters of *Treffpunkt im Unendlichen* are Sebastian, who bears the greatest resemblance to Klaus Mann; and Sonja, Sebastian's mistress, behind whom the figure of Erika Mann is readily discernible. The principal antagonist, Gregor Gregori, is consciously modelled after Gustaf Gründgens, Erika's erstwhile husband, whose relationship to Klaus and his writing will be discussed in detail later.[2] Psychologically more significant, however, is the fact that there are no less than two subordinate characters, in addition to Sebastian, who possess traits identifiable with Klaus Mann at various stages of his life: Peti, Sonja's fourteen-year-old brother, who plays a peripheral role in the novel and whose adolescent experiences are a direct blueprint of the author's descriptions of his adventures in the *Wilhelmsgymnasium*;[3] and Richard Darmstädter, a complex and tormented character, who commits suicide in Nice, in the wake of a dissolving homosexual relationship.

Sebastian, a writer and journalist who has met with limited success in his creative endeavors, is twenty-five years old, precisely the age of Klaus when he wrote the novel. In temperament and attitude he bears a strong resemblance to Andreas Magnus, but he generally lacks the excess of zeal and sense of mission which distinguishes the latter. He makes his first appearance embarking for Paris, where he remains for the better part of the work and where he is engaged to an aging dancer named Greta.

In parallel action, the remainder of the plot unfolds in Berlin, where a broad array of other significant characters play out their intricate roles. Among these is Sonja, a successful actress, caught up in an emotional triangle with Gregor Gregori, the vain, exhibitionistic dancer, totally intoxicated with his successes; and Privy Councillor Bayer, Sonja's rich, elderly benefactor, who is willing to have his wife committed to an institution in order to marry Sonja. Sonja, rather than Sebastian, can be considered the central character of the novel, since, at one time or another, she is intimately involved with most of the characters including Sebastian, who does not become part of the significant action until the end when he has a chance encounter with her. Other characters who contribute to the mood of the work, if not significantly to the plot, are Do and Froschele, the latter a Lesbian and morphine addict, both romantically involved with Gregor Gregori. Richard Darmstädter and Doktor Massis, a sinister type not heretofore seen in Klaus Mann's work, complete the circle of Berlin acquaintances.

Sonja is, relatively speaking, the most stable character in the novel. She has a precursor in Franziska of *Der fromme Tanz*, who, like Sonja, is not entirely devoid of emotional conflict, but accepts her privations with dignity and a certain level of maturity. Sonja, however, is destined for a more tragic fate. Her abrupt decision to embark on the journey which leads to her encounter with Sebastian is made under considerable psychological stress, caused in part by her need to escape the oppressive attentions of her suitor, Gregor Gregori. In this respect she resembles Suzanne Cobière, whose problematical relations with her benefactor, Mister Collan, are in some ways similar to Sonja's with Privy Councillor Bayer.

The figure of Richard Darmstädter, whose autobiographical significance has already been mentioned, deserves the most detailed interpretive scrutiny, not because his actions significantly affect the plot of the novel—he could just as easily have been left out altogether without altering the story—but because he relates to the author in a manner which cannot be understood solely from an artistic point of view. Although it bears some traits which are not typical of Klaus Mann, certain other aspects of Darmstädter's character are unmistakably autobiographical. The scion of a patrican Jewish family, Darmstädter displays many of the characteristics which Klaus ascribed to himself as a young man and which also pertain to some of the more highly-strung characters portrayed in his fiction: "Exaggerated in all his reactions and feelings, at times depressive, at times in love with life in a forced manner; very intelligent, but unstable; extravagantly sentimental and cynical; with a hunger for adventures, both physical (which in practice usually turned out to be rather second-class) and spiritual, superrational ones, which led him into mystical areas and uncontrollable ecstasies." (*Treffpunkt*, p. 206) Regarding the experiences of his youth, we are told: "The fifteen-year-old made his first suicide attempt for the sake of some

blond boy or other, who was in his class in Mainz. At that time he
went to a free country school in the Odenwald, where he felt better
for a time." (*Treffpunkt*, p. 207) Although the scene of his up-
bringing is moved from Munich to Mainz, and his family background is portrayed as Jewish, this description exactly fits the
young Klaus Mann. While there is no record of any attempted suicide when Klaus was fifteen, his own references to his depressive
moods and suicidal thoughts during and after his stay at the *Odenwaldschule* establish that he at least contemplated the act.

Even more significant of a similarity between Richard
Darmstädter and Klaus Mann than their backgrounds and personalities is the anticipatory nature of the entire Darmstädter episode.
The description of Darmstädter's suicide in Nice bears striking resemblance to Klaus's own suicide in Cannes some seventeen years
after the novel was written. Although little is known about the precise circumstances of his death, the psychological implications of
such an artistic portrayal and its possible unconscious relation to
the actual event should not be dismissed as mere "coincidence."

The second consciously autobiographical character in the work,
Sebastian, is, in some respects, a mirror image of Richard
Darmstädter. Although he possesses a similar artistic and intellectual bent, he is basically a much less volatile personality, with little
or no sign of the palpable emotional conflict which characterizes
the latter. Little information is given about his family background,
and the elaborate prehistory by means of which we acquire much
insight into the origins of Richard Darmstädter's problems is completely absent in Sebastian's case. While Darmstädter suffers under
the onus of a massive inferiority complex brought about by his ambivalent feelings toward his powerful, tyrannical father and complicated by his homosexuality, Sebastian possesses no such clearly
pronounced negative traits. In fact, Sebastian is, of all the characters in the novel with the possible exception of Sonja, relatively free
of conflict. Even after one of the climactic moments in the novel,
when his mistress is killed in an automobile accident, he pauses
briefly for a few slightly remorseful reflections and then continues
on his way to visit a friend. (*Treffpunkt*, p. 285)

The relationship between Sebastian and Sonja, which develops
after each has taken leave of a lover and has travelled to the less-
than-idyllic location of Fez, Morocco, has all the attributes of an
ideal union. After their harrowing experience with hashish, which

matches almost verbatim the description which Klaus gave of his and Erika's adventure with the drug in the same location a few years earlier, the couple appear to have fallen genuinely and deeply in love.[4] Shortly thereafter, Sonja contracts the mysterious fatal disease which ends their brief period of genuine happiness and fulfillment.

That the character of Sonja is modelled after Erika Mann is suggested not only by this last major episode in the novel and its relation to an actual event, but also by some significant remarks which Sebastian makes about what his lover's personality means to him. Soon after their first meeting, when it becomes evident that their mutual attraction is a great deal more than simple infatuation, the narration changes abruptly from third to first person, plural, and the mood becomes reflective and romantic: "We have various memories, and they seem to be the same.

"You must be my brother."

"You must be my sister."

"We have been preparing for each other so long, in order finally to become worthy of each other. We have scrutinized so many faces, in order finally to recognize each other's face." (*Treffpunkt*, p. 316) The author indulges in a bit of mystical predetermination as he enumerates the things which the couple have in common and makes a fleeting reference to Goethe's relations with Charlotte von Stein: "Ach, du warst in abgelebten Zeiten—." (*Treffpunkt*, p. 316)

Treffpunkt im Unendlichen, which has been largely overlooked in scholarship on Klaus Mann to date, is an important work, because it represents a transition from the author's early, largely experimental "Romantic" style to the more realistic narrative mode for which he is best known, the *Emigrantenroman* (Novel of Emigration). Like its predecessor, *Der fromme Tanz, Treffpunkt im Unendlichen* already possesses many of the attributes of the *Emigrantenroman*, even though its characters should not be considered emigrants in the strictest sense of the word, since they have not been forced to leave their country. Both novels, which take place in two or more major European cities, contain a host of disparate characters whose lives are loosely interwoven and whose common attributes are their personal loneliness and disorientation. Most of Klaus Mann's characters assumed the roles and characteristics of emigrants and displaced persons long before 1933, when the historical situation made the existence of such literary creations more in keeping with the times. While it cannot be denied that Klaus Mann had some intimations of the radical political changes which were about to take place in Germany at the time of writing and that the work itself contains some allusions thereto, it must be emphasized that the novel does not yet have the character of a political commentary; it is rather a description of a particular class of people in a specific social milieu, with which the author had been familiar for quite some time. That almost without exception the characters are drawn not only from persons with whom the author was intimately acquainted, but also from the world of art, literature, and the theater, should be noted.

It should also be kept in mind that the protagonists of the novel, Sonja and Sebastian, represent an idealized relationship which has been hinted at in previous works but never fully realized. Also significant is the fact that this ideal union endures for but a fleeting moment before tragedy strikes and the death of one of the partners dissolves it forever. Such an ending is consistent with those of the previous works in which one of the protagonists either dies or is abandoned by the other, leaving him in a state of tenuous optimism about his future happiness. Above all, the outcome of *Treffpunkt im Unendlichen* is consistent with those earlier works by virtue of the fact that lasting happiness has once again eluded its main character, and he is forced to face an uncertain future with no more moral or psychological reinforcement in his life than he had at the beginning.

II   Flucht in den Norden

On March 13, 1933, Klaus Mann left Germany, never to return as a German citizen. What caused him to leave barely a month and a half after Hitler's assumption of power was not so much the political necessity of the situation—the Mann family, with the exception of Klaus's uncle Heinrich, had not yet fallen into official disfavor with the Nazi Propagandists—but an all-consuming sense of contempt which he felt toward the perpetrators of the National Socialist nightmare: "We *could not* go back. Disgust would have killed us, disgust over our own wretchedness and the repugnant activity around us. The air in the Third Reich was unbreathable for certain lungs. Our homeland was threatened with suffocation.

A good, truly compelling reason to stay away." (*Wendepunkt*, p. 288)

In July, 1934, Klaus attended the International Writers' Congress in Moscow. His intention there was to speak out in favor of those intellectuals who stood in opposition to Fascism, not as a representative of any particular political ideology. In setting forth his reasons for attending the congress, he reiterated his basic disagreement with the proponents of Communism: "I am not a Communist and have never been one. I am also not a Marxist. I believe that the orthodox Marxists make many errors in many areas, moral, philosophical, psychological and political. But I do not believe that orthodox Marxism represents the greatest danger of the century. The greatest danger of the century is Fascism, which infects the easily susceptible masses with the poison of racial and nationalistic megalomania." (*Wendepunkt*, p. 326)

It was in 1934 that he wrote *Flucht in den Norden* (English version: Journey into Freedom), the first of his works which can legitimately be termed an *Emigrantenroman*. When viewed superficially, it is a simple story of a young woman torn between a sense of allegiance to her homeland, which is being threatened with political annihilation, and her attraction for a young man who has little understanding for her political sensitivities: "The classic conflict between love and duty, here it is experienced once again, with a naive vehemence, a youthful display of feeling, as if it were for the first time. But everything has already been there; my heroine, the boyish girl Johanna, confronts the same conflict with which many a patriot and many a revolutionary, many a soldier and many a priest has had to come to grips. Johanna, too, finally comes to grips with her classically tested and yet perpetually perplexing problem. She decides—in favor of duty, naturally." (*Wendepunkt*, pp. 331-32)

Klaus Mann's rather facile commentary masks many of the deeper implications which his novel contains. The manifest political theme, along with the classic conflict of duty and inclination, should not draw the reader's attention away from the deeper, psychological meaning inherent in it; nor should it obscure the many aspects which it shares with the author's previous, less politically motivated work. What is at first striking about Klaus Mann's statement and the aspect of the work to which it alludes is the description of the main character, Johanna. The reference to her as "the boyish girl" and her "youthful display of feeling" once again point to the fact that youth and childhood and the specific imagery which they convey continued to exert a special influence on the author's aesthetic and ideological sensibilities. Johanna's resemblance to a young boy, which is frequently mentioned in the work, is further evidence of the author's bisexual orientation. Ragnar, her lover, whose attractiveness and manly attributes are never in question, is also singled out for his youthful characteristics: "Youth from the image on a vase, large body, breathing and hairy, legs spread, face laughing, youth with the prominent member ... strength in his legs, he laughs still, strength in his arms, as he raises the pitcher, pours cold water into the washbasin ...: youth, raising the pitcher, youth, immersing his head in cold water...." (*Flucht*, p. 236)

The earlier work which bears the closest resemblance to *Flucht in den Norden*, the novella *Abenteuer des Brautpaars*, has so many similar features that it could be considered a miniature prototype of the novel. Aside from the fact that the principal scene of action in both works is Scandinavia, the main aspect which both have in common is the political activity of the protagonists. Jak, the dedicated Communist of the former, is transformed into Johanna, the equally dedicated anti-Fascist of the latter. While Jak renounces an intense political career in his homeland in favor of a life of aimless wandering and adventure, Johanna renounces her aimless wandering and adventure in favor of a life of intense political activity in her homeland. The single common motivation which links the diametrically opposite actions of both characters is the necessity for some form of "flight." In the one, it acts as a means of escaping responsibility; in the other, as a vehicle for returning to it. The monumental journey into the northernmost reaches of Scandinavia which Johanna and Ragnar undertake on impulse, and which comprises much of the latter half of the novel, is a symbol of the incurable restlessness in their spirits and the lack of fulfillment in their lives. The suggestion that, once having reached their illusory goal, they continue their journey to Iceland, is agreed to by Johanna, until she learns of her trusted comrade Bruno's arrest in Germany and his almost certain death at the hands of the Nazis. At that point, she makes up her mind, suddenly and resolutely, to pursue the dictates of her conscience. The end of the novel, which almost immediately follows this drastic turn of events, contains an undercurrent of fatalism which is to some degree present in earlier works, along with a sense of guilt and despair which has been noted in

similar contexts. Like Andreas Magnus and others of his ilk,
Johanna is troubled by feelings of guilt over her desire to abandon
her ideals and succumb to her natural inclinations. Unlike the former, however, who continues optimistically to pursue his vague and
undefinable objective, Johanna makes up her mind to renounce her
desires and complete her higher mission, heedless of the consequences:

"What do you want to do now," said Ragnar. "Now no choice is left to
me, said Johanna—" she cried no more. "Now I have the example.—Perhaps he despised me while he was dying," she added, after a pause . . .
    "That is not true," said Ragnar—they stood across from one another.
"The history of the world consists of futile sacrifices and wasted faith."
    "That is not the consideration which is appropriate to the living,"
Johanna answered him. "We no longer are entitled to this consideration.
We no longer have a choice. Our entire heroism will be not to go under be-
fore our fate demands it." (*Flucht*, pp. 316-17)

Although, for his part, Ragnar does not share Johanna's political concerns, his temperament does not markedly differ from hers.
He, too, is given to fits of moodiness and depression, which signal
the presence of a certain hostility and rebelliousness lurking not far
beneath the surface of his otherwise placid nature. Both openly reveal an infatuation with, if not a longing for, death:

[Ragnar]: "Death cannot be bad. Life is bad, yes, that is the surprise. We
were not prepared for it. We imagined it to be easier, or at least of a more
beautiful sadness. I believe now that death will more likely happen to us as
a pleasant surprise."
    "There are hours—when I would *so like* to die," said Johanna from be-
low, her face resting quietly against his knees. "I have never told that to
anyone, but I am telling it to you. I often think that I would rather die than
anything else. Just not to have to move my hand anymore . . ." (*Flucht*,
p. 298)

Sentiments of this kind are reminiscent of those voiced by the very
youthful characters of Klaus Mann's earliest works. It may be recalled that Harald, one of the main characters in *Die Jungen* and a
prototype for the many figures in subsequent works who bear an
autobiographical relation to the author, expresses himself in a similar manner. So, too, does Anja, who represents essentially the same

spirit of rebelliousness and morbidity which is so strongly characteristic of the early works.

An additional thematic element, the significance of which is that
it provides a direct link to the earliest work, is the appearance of a
horse with strikingly beautiful features, which suddenly gallops in
front of Ragnar's car and nearly causes a fatal accident: ". . . with
flying flanks and high-stepping front feet it danced, whinnying
stridently, trumpeting in its overpowering irrationality, intoxicated
by its own movements, completely beautiful in its noble helpless-
ness." (*Flucht*, p. 301) Immediately after the incident, the image of
the horse is associated in Johanna's mind with another death wish:
" 'Why can't this be the last picture which is allotted to me? It
would be a great picture. Why couldn't it go badly this time, automobile accident in the far North—Ragnar was usually so reliably
uncoordinated. I would like to die. . . .' " (*Flucht*, p. 302) A similar depiction of a horse occurs in the orgiastic dream scene of "Kaspar Hausers Traum von Morgen," which immediately precedes the
final episode describing Kaspar Hauser's funeral. Here, once
again, an image of stark beauty, an embodiment of life in its most
vibrant form, becomes linked with thoughts of death. Both extremes coexist almost as a single indivisible entity, an essential component of Klaus Mann's early work which persists, virtually unal-
tered, in his literature of exile.

Other aspects of Ragnar's character which relate him to similar
characterizations in the early works are the expressions of hostility
toward his father and the general distrust of authority which he
consistently exhibits. In the course of their journey to the North,
Ragnar reveals to Johanna a dream in which his father appears in
riding apparel and beats his mother with a horsewhip. Like characters in the early work who describe a male parent who in the past
has tormented or persecuted them in some way, he describes his
feelings about his father, now deceased: " 'Did something like that
really happen?' " asked Johanna, who had become very pale.

" 'Not exacly that,' he interjected bleakly. 'That he beat her with
the horsewhip, no, I never saw that. But she suffered under him
every day, every day he had a new atrocity ready for her, he tormented her horribly—very horribly. . . . That is why I hated my
father,' he said slowly, stressing every syllable." (*Flucht*, p. 383)

Johanna, too, has a problematical family background, which, although somewhat more stable than that of Ragnar, can be con-

sidered the source of some of her present unhappiness. Her father, a man of some artistic sensibilities, was also prey to libertine urges during the early part of his marriage; and her mother, in apparent retaliation to her husband's infidelity, rather late in life began an affair with a dentist named Dr. Kücken, which ended only after a comparatively long period of self-reproach and suicidal guilt on her part. Both parents profess pacifistic tendencies, especially the mother, an avowed Pan-Europeanist, who spends much of her time giving public lectures on the subject, a practice which could only make the family suspect in politically sensitive Germany and increases Johanna's worries about their welfare. Her brother Georg, a Communist, is engaged in illicit political activities which have the effect of threatening the family's security still more. Oddly, it is only after Georg's friend Bruno enters the scene that Johanna herself begins to take active interest in her brother's cause.

The only other significant character in the novel is Johanna's friend Karin, who was in part responsible for her leaving Germany in the first place. She, too, has a history of family troubles, having lost both a father and a fiancé in the course of events. Her significance fades rapidly during the second half of the novel, after Johanna rejects her in favor of Ragnar. The Lesbian relationship which develops early between them adds another example to the stock of characters in Klaus Mann's novels who are either homosexual or bisexual. Aside from participating in this interlude, Karin does not significantly contribute to the central theme of the novel. Another minor character, Yvonne, provides the story with a welcome bit of comic relief and is an interesting caricature of a scatterbrained, hysterical personality; but she too has relatively little importance for the plot as a whole.

Although the conflict which involves the main character is manifestly related to the political situation in central Europe during the early 1930's, it would be a gross oversimplification to consider it the only important motivating factor in the novel. The author's conscious intent in structuring the work as he did was not merely to create a story about people forced to deal with a certain historical necessity, but to construct certain personalities whose conflicts are of universal interest and whose problems transcend any particular historical circumstances:

This is what the inventors of stories are like! They delight in the moral distress and sensual weakness of their creations, only to abandon the poor, invented characters disdainfully as soon as the problematical, sinful escapade is over and life begins in earnest. The good anti-Fascist Johanna, who starves and conspires with her comrade in a musty Parisian hotel room, is no longer interesting. But the inwardly torn, upset Johanna, the lascivious Amazon and pugnacious courtesan, the lover with the bad conscience, the heroic girl with the penchant for intoxicatingly excessive sexuality—I liked her, she was to me an object of psychological curiosity and poetically human sympathy. (*Wendepunkt*, p. 332)

Although autobiographical elements are less readily apparent in this novel than in *Treffpunkt im Unendlichen*, at least as they apply to the formation of specific characters, some aspects of Klaus Mann's life concurrent with the writing of the work lie in its background. The figure of Johanna is consciously modelled after Annemarie Schwarzenbach, who was the common acquaintance of both Klaus and Erika and their long-time friend Ricki Hallgarten, and who was intended to be the fourth passenger on their ill-fated motor trip to Persia. The Scandinavian trip which constitutes the major portion of the novel is based on a similar trip which Klaus and Erika made in 1931.[5]

While *Flucht in den Norden* does not rank among Klaus Mann's most carefully constructed works—by his own admission, he wrote it rather effortlessly—its main significance lies in the fact that he was able to combine already familiar subject matter—the theme of "flight"—with an uncanny perception of the social and political realities of his time. Christopher Isherwood gives an indication of just how sensitive—and in a real sense, prophetic—Klaus was, when he cites Klaus's reference to the work, which he was in the process of writing, as "a pre-war novel."[6] The political situation which Johanna and her associates are confronting is an accurate representation of the gloomy events which had already taken place in Europe, and, at the same time, a foreshadowing of the even more distressing situation to come.

The characters in the novel represent almost every type of "young European intellectual" which several years earlier the author had envisioned in his essays and fiction. Johanna is an example of the politically aware activist with slight Marxist tendencies. Ragnar is her opposite, generally apathetic, politically naive and devoid of purpose. The circle is completed with another secondary character, Ragnar's brother Jens, who represents the most dangerous element among the youth of the time: the young proto-Fascist, who openly espouses the ideals of National Socialism. The work is at once a reflection of how deeply Klaus Mann felt about the dangers inherent in the contemporary European situation and how powerless he was to do anything about them. Such feelings are expressed in Johanna's thoughts at the novel's conclusion:

Johanna, the boyish girl who would rather die, must accept what she today, with head held high, calls her fate—what will it be? . . . Will you experience victory, and will it look the way one fantasizes victories—if it finally comes? Small hotel rooms in Paris, Prague and Zurich will be the showplace of your destiny. You will speak at meetings and write in newspapers; you will act as a courier and perhaps distribute illegal material in Germany, and perhaps even be shot, but first tormented and jeered; or you will still participate in the Great World War, indeed, perhaps even survive it, but that is improbable; and for a long time you will be homeless, but by no means free, but rather dependent on your poverty and the orders of a mysteriously concealed party leadership . . . You have no choice, Johanna, you must accept this, since death does not want you. Go, take it upon yourself, pull out, you are brave; guard against doubts, close your heart to them, or else you will break down. Be pious and strong. (*Flucht*, pp. 317-18)

These somber pronouncements, combined with an element of faint optimism, are reminiscent of the endings of other works by Klaus Mann. The essential difference, however, lies in the fact that an element of historical reality which was to have a profound influence on the author himself provides the background for the heroine's dilemma. In *Der fromme Tanz*, we saw a hero who possessed many of his author's attributes enter a new phase of his life with an attitude similar to that of Johanna. Here, too, in the description of Johanna's future activities, we are privy to a series of events which, in many respects, parallel those activities which Klaus Mann was engaged in at the time and was destined to pursue for most of the remainder of his life.

An interesting variation of the central theme of *Flucht in den Norden* is contained in the short story *Letztes Gespräch* (Last Conversation), which Klaus published in June, 1934, in *Die Sammlung*, the journal which he then edited. It depicts the plight of a pair of German expatriates, Karl and Annette, who are living in Paris, where their exile has left them in a state of moral and psychological bankruptcy. Karl finds the opportunity to raise himself out of this

spiritual limbo by joining a group of young Communists dedicated
to the defeat of Fascism, led by a youth named Bruno—who, not
coincidentally, bears the same name and has the same function as
his counterpart in *Flucht in den Norden*. Annette, however, rejects
this activist approach as a solution to their problems; and her refusal to join Karl and his friends leads to their separation and her
eventual decision to commit suicide.

Karl is motivated by the same principles of political *engagement*
as Johanna, but lacks her fatalistic outlook and melancholy temperament. Annette, in contrast, resembles Johanna in temperament, but allows her desire for oblivion, her death wish, to become
the dominant force in her life. She represents what Johanna might
have become had she continued on the course which she and Ragnar had set for themselves: "The overpowering love for death,
which did not make her face bitter, but transfigured it in a friendly
way, encompassed her true love for her husband and friend."[7] Her
choice of death over life in the context of her particular situation
provides a fitting counterpoint to the final scenes of *Flucht in den
Norden* and a possible alternative conclusion to the novel.

III   Die Sammlung

On the first of September, 1933, scarcely more than five months
after the beginning of Klaus Mann's term of exile, the first issue of
his journal, *Die Sammlung* (The Concentration) was published.
Originally intended to be based in Zurich, the journal found its permanent home in Amsterdam, under the auspices of the newly
formed Querido publishing house, which was headed by Fritz
Landshoff, a long-time friend of Klaus Mann. *Die Sammlung*
quickly became one of the leading voices of the German intelligentsia in exile and was to embroil its editor and a number of its
contributors in a political controversy, which none of them could
have envisioned at the outset.

On the first page of the first issue, Klaus Mann set forth the philosophy and purpose of the journal in order to make its readers
aware of the nature and sentiment of the writings which it would
contain:

This periodical will serve literature, that is: that high concern which tou-
ches not just one people, but all peoples on earth. Some people, however,

have become so confused that they insult their best people, are ashamed of them and will not tolerate them in their own country. In such countries, literature is being raped; in order to avoid rape, it flees such a country. The true, valid German literature is in this situation; that, namely, which cannot remain silent before the degradation of its people and the outrage which is perpetrated upon itself. The will to oppose, by itself, forces it into battle. Even its appearance, even the names of those who represent it, become a declaration of war on the enemy.

A literary periodical is not a political one; the chronicle of day-to-day events, the analysis of them or the prediction of those to come does not make up its content. Nevertheless, today it will have a political mission. Its position must be unequivocal. Whoever takes the trouble to follow our periodical should have no doubt as to where we, the editors, and where our colleagues stand. From the beginning, it will be clear where we hate and where we hope to love.—

That *Die Sammlung* was to be a literary journal was made clear from the beginning; what Klaus Mann added in his manifesto, and what was apparently not clear to all those who were asked or who volunteered to contribute to the journal was its firm political stance, which became more consolidated as subsequent issues were released. Although considerable space was devoted to literary criticism, some written by the editor himself, the first issues contained numerous articles of an analytical and clearly anti-Nazi nature, including a provocative piece by Klaus's uncle Heinrich, entitled "Sittliche Erziehung durch deutsche Erhebung" (Moral Education through German Uplifting). Heinrich Mann, who, along with Aldous Huxley and André Gide, had been listed among the journal's original patrons, had already earned the disfavor of the Third Reich's guardians of intellectual purity because of his leftist leanings and had been expelled from the Prussian Academy of the Arts in February, 1933. Shortly thereafter, he emigrated to France.

The first issue also contained a list of future contributors, among whom were Thomas Mann, René Schickele, Stefan Zweig and Alfred Döblin, all writers of prominence in Germany at the time, who had also emigrated but continued to keep close ties with their homeland. On October 10, 1933, the *Reichsstelle zur Förderung des deutschen Schrifttums* (National Authority for the Promotion of German Literature) published the list in a trade periodical, *Das Börsenblatt für den deutschen Buchhandel,* and included a warning about German literary periodicals in exile, *Die Sammlung* in partic-

ular: "The literary emigration periodicals in the various countries
to the west, east and southeast of us are increasing. It is necessary
that the German bookseller watches them closely, gets to know
them and warns people about their proliferation in Germany;
warns them even when the periodicals in question are not yet for-
bidden, because, if he distributes them, he becomes guilty of intellectual treason."[8] Not long after this announcement appeared, the
Börsenblatt published a series of telegrams from Thomas Mann,
Schickele and Döblin in which the respective authors denied knowledge of the political character of *Die Sammlung* and withdrew their
association with the journal. Thomas Mann's terse telegraphed
statement can be considered typical of the others as well: "Can
only confirm that the character of the first issue of *Die Sammlung*
does not correspond to its original program. Thomas Mann."[9]
Stefan Zweig had already written a letter disavowing his collaboration with the journal before the publication of the list of contributors by the *Börsenblatt*.

These declarations, which alarmed many German writers and intellectuals already in exile and which earned their authors considerable additional notoriety in the exile press, seem too superficial not
to warrant further inquiry into the reasons for their appearance.
There was never any doubt that the writers in question actually
wrote them and that they were not simply fabrications of a politically sensitive and unscrupulous Nazi propaganda machine. What
was not clear at the outset was that the publishing houses with
which these writers were associated—the S. Fischer Verlag, in the
case of Thomas Mann, Schickele and Döblin, and the Insel Verlag
in the case of Zweig—had, for political reasons, solicited statements of disassociation from *Die Sammlung* from the various writers in question and had allowed them to be published for the most
part without the writers' knowledge or approval.

From the publishers' point of view, their action was warranted
by circumstances. Both Fischer and Insel were well-established concerns whose market for publication was, and had been since their
inception, almost exclusively German. The rapidly deteriorating
political situation after 1933 forced them to remain at best politically neutral or face the prospect of having to move into exile themselves. Because the latter alternative was, for various reasons, impracticable, they chose the former and, in so doing, attempted to

demonstrate the supposed political purity of the major writers under their aegis.

The writers' motivations for making the statements in the first place are diverse and more complicated. Schickele's main defense of his action was his fear, largely unjustified, that Samuel Fischer, founder of the firm and already an old man at the time, would be physically harmed by the Nazis if his association with *Die Sammlung* were made public.[10] Zweig attempted to remain politically neutral, although his private sympathies clearly remained on the side of the exiles. His book *Erasmus of Rotterdam*, a chapter of which was to have appeared in *Die Sammlung*, paints the portrait of a great figure in an equally turbulent time, whose greatness lay in the fact that he was able to create a Humanism without siding with either of the extreme factions of the period, the Reformation on the one hand, the Catholic Church on the other. In a letter to Klaus Mann, dated September 18, 1933, Zweig attempted to justify his refusal to contribute to *Die Sammlung*: "Were your newspaper, dear Klaus Mann, really only a representation of our achievement, our activity and will, without any polemical overtones, I would gladly have participated. But for seven months or even longer, just like your father, I have not published one work in a domestic or foreign paper because I believe that if we give no cause to turn the facts around, the injustice would become clearer and indisputable, and they would not be able to turn the spear around and say that we have provoked them."[11] Döblin's rejection of *Die Sammlung* is contradicted by his subsequent actions. Rather than disassociate himself entirely from the exile press, he submitted a number of writings to Querido, publisher of *Die Sammlung*, and a piece of his even appeared in *Die Sammlung* itself, in June, 1934. It is probable that Döblin simply sent his telegram of disavowal as a favor to Fischer, without bothering to search for a more elaborate justification.

Thomas Mann's justification is more complex and carefully reasoned, although, in the final analysis, no more efficacious than the others. His book, *Die Geschichten Jaakobs* (The Stories of Jacob), the first volume of his monumental *Joseph* tetralogy, had just been published at the urging of Gottfried Bermann Fischer, son-in-law of the founder and then publisher of the S. Fischer-Verlag. Thomas Mann had seriously considered having the book published outside Germany by Querido, but apparently changed his mind when he became persuaded that its publication inside Germany would have a more beneficial effect on the German people than its publication outside Germany, where it would never reach them: "If it succeeds, if the public in Germany makes a success of this book, the work of an outlaw and a work whose contents offend, without the powers that be daring to prevent it—one has to admit that that would be much more proper and pleasant, much more annoying for the powers that be, a more striking victory over them than an entire barrage of emigrant polemics."[12] Whatever the reasons, Thomas Mann's decision to continue publication of his work in Germany and his consequent reluctance to let himself be counted among the professed writers in exile subjected him to sharp criticism from the exile press and even moved some of the members of his own family, Heinrich and Erika in particular, to urge him to express himself publicly on the subject. Klaus, who remained uncharacteristically restrained in his public involvement in the matter, tried privately to persuade his father to cast his lot with the exiles. It was not until February, 1936, after Eduard Korrodi of the *Neuer Zürcher Zeitung* launched an attack on the entire exile literature, in which he alleged that it was dominated by Jewish influences, that Thomas Mann sent a letter to the same newspaper vehemently defending the writers in exile and publicly declaring his support of them. On February 12, 1936, he lost his German citizenship.

In the meantime, *Die Sammlung* continued to function without the support of some of its more illustrious contributors, until it succumbed to financial difficulties in August, 1935, exactly two years after it had begun publication. It was largely due to the efforts of its publisher, Fritz Landshoff, that the journal lasted as long as it did. During its short span of existence, however, it published the literary and political viewpoints of such diverse minds as Albert Einstein, Franz Kafka, Ernst Toller, Jean Cocteau, Ernest Hemingway, André Gide, Aldous Huxley and Leon Trotsky. It remains today one of the most significant voices of the progressive German intelligentsia during the period of moral and intellectual anarchy which characterizes the formative years of the Third Reich.

IV   Symphonie Pathétique

One year after *Flucht in den Norden* was published, Klaus

Mann's second biographical novel, *Symphonie Pathétique*, appeared. An artistic rendition of the great composer Tchaikcvsky's last years, it represents something of a departure from the youth-oriented political prose of the author's own youth and as such bears a closer resemblance to *Alexander* than to any other major work of his exile. In the case of the latter it has been noted that Klaus's choice of hero was in part determined by his perception of the historical Alexander's excess of zeal in the pursuit of his goal and his massive sense of inadequacy and disappointment upon the realization that his dream would fall far short of being fulfilled, A similar dichotomy in the personality of Tchaikovsky forms the particular combination of artistic talent and immense inner conflict which so fascinated Klaus Mann: "His neurotic unrest, his complexes and his ecstasies, his anxieties and his peaks of emotion, the almost unbearable loneliness in which he had to live, the pain, which he wanted again and again to see transformed into melody, into beauty — I could describe it all, none of it was foreign to me." (*Wendepunkt*, p. 333)

Coupled with this interest in exploring the inner life of a particularly dynamic historical individual was for Klaus a strong sense of identification with his hero, perhaps because he perceived aspects of his own personality which he had in common with Tchaikovsky. One of these was homosexuality,[13] another was the sense of perennial homelessness, a self-imposed exile, already noted as an attribute of other Klaus Mann characters, which now takes on an added significance in relation to the real exile to which Klaus was then being forced to submit: "A 'man without a country'—my great, moving friend Peter Ilyitch was that in more than one sense. Not only his *eros* isolated him, made him an outsider, almost a pariah; also his kind of talent, his artistic style was too mixed, too vibrant, too cosmopolitan to be entirely palatable anywhere.... He was an emigrant, an exile, not for political reasons, but because he never felt at home anywhere. He suffered everywhere." (*Wendepunkt*, p. 332)

Also significant for the novel in its relation to previous works is the continued evidence of the close association which Klaus Mann establishes between the troubled lives of his main characters and their deaths. In a passage from *Der Wendepunkt*, in which he makes one of the very few references to his own homosexuality, he cites Platen's well-known phrase, "Wer die Schönheit angeschaut mit Augen—ist dem Tode schon anheimgegeben." (*Symphonie Pathétique*, pp. 333-34) ("He who has looked at beauty with his eyes is already delivered up to death.") This reference is made not only to Tchaikovsky, but also to Herman Bang, another "man without a country" who ranked high in Klaus's pantheon of artistic deities—and finally, by implication, to himself.

Klaus Mann's association of homosexuality and death may account for an error which he makes with regard to a basic fact about Tchaikovsky's life—one so well-known that one is tempted to conclude that Klaus deliberately misrepresented it—that his death was not a suicide. The historical Tchaikovsky died of cholera; Klaus Mann portrays him deliberately swallowing the glass of water which produced the onset of the disease: "There is no consolation. The disconsolate, famous Peter Ilyitch will die his disconsolate, furtive death; he commits suicide, with cunning discretion, as a fifty-three-year-old. 'Brief pilgrimage — whom does it tire? Me already too long: Pain tires. . . .' So it was with Stefan George; also one who knew the affliction of *eros*." (*Wendepunkt*, p. 334) It would seem that Klaus Mann deliberately distorted the facts surrounding the circumstances of his hero's death in order to dramatize the suffering which was a part of his life. There is also a firm connection between the suffering of Tchaikovsky and other Klaus Mann characters and their homosexuality.

Evidence of Klaus Mann's continued fascination with the unique problems of youth and childhood is manifested in his strong emphasis on Tchaikovsky's relations with his young nephew, Vladimir Davidov, nicknamed "Bob", in whom he saw not only an object of Tchaikovsky's deepest feelings of love and admiration, but also a reflection of many of the composer's own attributes, his talents as well as his profoundest fears and insecurities:

For even young Vladimir already knew depressed, bitterly despondent hours; he knew nervous anxieties, melancholy, hatred, and the most oppressive feeling of inferiority. On the other hand, he was anxious to please people, to win their hearts through a lovable and agreeable presence. Only all these traits were less clearly and disturbingly apparent in young Bob than in the highly excitable Peter Ilyitch: the youth and supple charm of the rapidly grown-up page had the power to reconcile all the opposites of his being, to ameliorate the problems, to smooth out the contradictions, to transform the erratic or tormented into the gracious. (*Symphonie Pathétique*, p. 214)

Tchaikovsky's Sixth Symphony, which was dedicated to Vladimir Davidov and from which the title of the novel is derived, is portrayed as the composer's *magnum opus*, the culmination of a life of toil and suffering and a symbol of the passions and torments which accompanied the creation of all his art. Klaus Mann sought to portray this final achievement in much the same way as he had portrayed Alexander's conquests; as historical achievements of almost infinite magnitude, brought about by two personalities who at bottom made unrealistic estimates of their own capabilities and harbored distorted images of their true worth as human beings.

V   Mephisto

Mephisto, published in 1936, is perhaps Klaus Mann's most controversial novel and therefore his best-known work. While it is not necessarily his best work from an artistic point of view, it deserves special consideration in any study of Klaus Mann's total work because of its unique origin and intent. Subtitled *Roman einer Karriere* (Novel of a Career), it is the story of a talented, but vain and ambitious actor who rises to the pinnacle of success in the Third Reich and attains a position of power and influence far out of proportion to his real value as a person. He achieves his success often at the expense of other persons, whom he uses as stepping-stones to further his ambition and discards when they are no longer of use to him.

The initial and continued controversy over the novel originated from the description of the main character, Hendrik Höfgen, who bears a striking resemblance to Gustaf Gründgens, whom Klaus met when they were both performing in his play *Anja und Esther* in Hamburg in the fall of 1925. It was there that Gründgens met Erika Mann, who was also acting in the play. They were married, and after Gründgens became a Nazi and remained in Germany, later divorced. Klaus's feelings about his erstwhile brother-in-law were mixed from the beginning. Although he acknowledged Gründgens's apparent gifts, he found fault with what he perceived to be the actor's extreme vanity and his compulsion to win other people's admiration: "He suffered from his vanity as if from a

wound. It was this feverish, impassioned coquetry which gave his
being the verve, the impetus, on which he also literally seemed to
consume himself. How deep must the inferiority complex be which
seeks to compensate itself in such fireworks of charm. What unrest,
what tormented mistrust is concealed behind this exalted mirthful-
ness." (*Wendepunkt*, p. 162)

These traits, as well as some of Gründgens's more apparent physical characteristics, are incorporated in the character of Hendrik
Höfgen—the similarity even extends to the names, with the repeti-
tion of the initials, the umlauted vowels in the same relative position, and the same number of syllables in each name. Most of the
other characters also have their counterparts in real people who
were common acquaintances of both Gründgens and Klaus Mann
and who figured prominently in the artistic and theatrical life of
Germany in the late 1920's and early 1930's: the stage director, Max
Reinhardt, the actresses Elisabeth Bergner and Therese Giehse, the
writers Carl Sternheim and Gottfried Benn, to name a few. Even
Members of Klaus's own family and his circle of intimate acquaintances are represented.

Mephisto was first published serially in the *Pariser Tageszeitung*
in June, 1936. Because of the apparent similarity between so many
characters in the novel and real persons, the editors referred to it as
a *Schlüsselroman* (a novel in which living persons appear under
feigned names). In a letter to the editors of the *Pariser Tageszeitung*
written shortly after this reference appeared, Klaus Mann vehemently took issue with their use of the term *Schlüsselroman* and
provided the following explanation for the obvious similarity between the main character and Gründgens, to whom he did not refer
by name: "It was *not* my intent to tell the story of a certain person
when I wrote *Mephisto, Novel of a Career*. It was my intent to portray a *type*, and along with it the various milieus . . . the sociological and intellectual preconditions which made its ascendency possible in the first place."[14]

More than a decade later, in the final version of his autobiography, *Der Wendepunkt*, Klaus once again refers to the novel;
and, although he mentions Gründgens by name, he maintains essentially the same position he took in 1936 to explain the novel's
purpose:

Is the privy councillor and director Hendrik Höfgen, whose novel I wrote, a portrait of the privy councillor and director Gustaf Gründgens, with whom I was acquainted as a young man? Not quite. Höfgen differs in many ways from my former brother-in-law. But even assuming that the character in the novel were more similar to the original than he actually is, Gründgens could still not be considered the "hero" of the book. It is, in this attempt at contemporary social criticism, not at all a question of the individual instance, but of the type. Someone else could just as well have served as an example. My choice fell on Gründgens—not because I considered him particularly bad (he was probably better than many another dignitary of the Third Reich), but simply because I happened to know him particularly well. (*Wendepunkt*, p. 335)

It is difficult for a neutral observer to distinguish Klaus's possible prior antipathy to his former brother-in-law from his social conscience, which may have justified the kind of indignation expressed by such a highly unflattering portrait of an actor who rises to power and influence in the Third Reich. While Hendrik Höfgen's career parallels that of Gustaf Gründgens in its more general attributes, certain unsavory details such as Höfgen's sadomasochistic affair with a mulatto dancer named Juliette are, for the most part, gratuitous and do little more than titillate the reader, drawing his attention away from the novel's more serious satirical purpose. Legitimate questions can be raised as to Klaus's wisdom in selecting as his model a person so closely associated with his personal life and making him the focus of attention of the entire novel. Despite the author's assertions to the contrary, Höfgen is the main character, and his personality overshadows that of any other character in the book. Hermann Göring and Joseph Goebbels, who might legitimately bear the brunt of the author's criticism, appear only briefly, Hitler is mentioned in passing.

Whatever Klaus Mann's conscious or unconscious intentions in choosing Gründgens as a model for his *Mephisto* may have been, his tendency to create his characters from persons he personally knew had been established long before he wrote the work in question. In his two articles on *Mephisto,* Werner Rieck points out that the character of Hendrik Höfgen has a predecessor in that of Gregor Gregori of *Treffpunkt im Unendlichen*, and that the latter work is, in most respects, as much a *Schlüsselroman* as *Mephisto*;[15] this despite the fact that *Treffpunkt im Unendlichen* had been written before the Nazis came to power and has no satirical or political intent whatsoever. It is perhaps unfortunate that Klaus Mann's first

major work intended to have serious political impact gained its
considerable notoriety for the wrong reasons. After World War II,
Klaus made repeated attempts to have the book reprinted in Germany. He never succeeded while he was alive. Gründgens remained
an influential figure in German theatrical circles even after the war,
and publishers were reluctant to open old personal, as well as political wounds. Even as late as 1966, court proceedings were success-
fully instituted by Gründgens's adopted son, Peter Gorski-Gründ-
gens, to ban the publication of *Mephisto* in Germany.[16] The memory of Gustaf Gründgens, the actor, continued to overshadow the
memory of the political events upon which he had had a small but
palpable impact.

When viewed in the context of Klaus Mann's total *oeuvre*,
Mephisto is both a historical and artistic anomaly. As his first and
only attempt at political satire, it represents a departure from the
kind of works he had become accustomed to writing during the
period of his exile before the beginning of World War II. These
works were of two basic types: biographical novels about significant historical or artistic individuals, and heavily autobiographical
works dealing with the problems of the emigration. Although
Mephisto applies some of the techniques used in both these types,
in its end result it represents neither. It must be considered a unique
phenomenon in the evolution of Klaus Mann's art, an attempt to
penetrate new and different artistic dimensions which failed in the
final analysis.

VI   Vergittertes Fenster

Klaus Mann's last work of fiction based on a historical character
is *Vergittertes Fenster* (Barred Window), which was published in
1937. In *Der Wendepunkt*, Klaus gives the following précis of its
contents:

Vergittertes Fenster deals with the death of a man, or actually with his
death wish, his flight into darkness. The tragic hero whom I chose this
time was King Ludwig the Second of Bavaria, not the charmed fairy-tale
prince and picturesque Lohengrin who was idolized by his people and
praised lyrically by the Parisian Symbolists; but rather the marked, lost
one, the victim of secret intrigues and his own *hybris*, the psychopath, the
martyr, a prince of passion, more like the late Oscar Wilde than a

Wagnerian hero: already somewhat decayed, already deformed, with bad teeth and puffy lips, with a look that naturally remained handsome and a still very majestic demeanor. Thus I described him, his memories (in which the brightness of Lohengrin still ought to be affirmed in retrospect), his last ecstasies, his dignity in downfall, his clearsightedness in paranoid eclipse. (*Wendepunkt*, p. 370)

Following the pattern of many of Klaus's earliest works, *Vergittertes Fenster* is a novella, written in the concise, highly descriptive style which characterizes the genre. As such, it stands in sharp contrast to the lengthy novels, with their wealth of characterization and plot detail which highlight this particular phase of his career. Equally atypical of Klaus Mann's work of the period is the fact that portions of the novella are written in the first person, utilizing a technique which approaches stream of consciousness much more closely than any other work of his encountered thus far. An attempt is made to reproduce Ludwig's innermost thoughts as he is gradually engulfed by the madness which ultimately leads to his death.

Declared hopelessly insane by his doctors, Ludwig is brought to one of his many opulent residences in Bavaria, Castle Berg on Lake Starnberg, and placed in the permanent custody of his psychiatrist, Dr. von Gudden. Every effort is made to give the mad king the impression that there is nothing wrong with him and that he is being treated with the deference appropriate to his station, but the barred window in his chamber betrays the reality of his present situation. The bulk of the novella describes the king's solitary reminiscences, as he spends his final hours heatedly reliving the recent events in his life. He reviews his passionate relationship with his protegé Richard Wagner, now dead, to whom he dedicated a series of opulent residences, the construction of which nearly bankrupted the state of Bavaria. He recalls his troubled friendship with his cousin Elisabeth, Empress of Austria, and his love for her sister, Sophie, and his clandestine affair with a young actor named Joseph Kainz. The climax of the story occurs when Ludwig lures his protector, Dr. von Gudden, down to the lake on the pretext of wanting to go for a walk. Ludwig enters the water and the physician follows in an attempt to rescue him. After a protracted struggle, in which Ludwig is determined to share his own death with his supposed benefactor, they both drown.

Klaus Mann evidently intended to write the novella as a diversion from the more complex narratives of the period, a need which would find its most articulate expression the following year in his last major work, *Der Vulkan*. *Vergittertes Fenster* was written rather quickly and effortlessly, as were many of his shorter prose works, while Klaus was a guest at the home of Annemarie Schwarzenbach in Engadin, Switzerland:

Even if it is not a presumptuous story, the curious choice of material does seem to me to evidence a certain coarse audacity, which is not far from presumption. Because it still is somewhat curious when an author, who knows and recognizes his political and moral obligation, permits himself such an escapade, a cheerful excursion into the melancholic-aesthetic, into dear old familiar-morbid fairyland. *Escapism*, the austere word, with which a puritanic-progressive Anglo-Saxon literary criticism perhaps too frequently operates, seems here for once really appropriate. (*Wendepunkt*, p. 370)

Despite the fact that Klaus belittles the novella's significance in relation to what he considered to be his primary literary goals, *Vergittertes Fenster* is, in many respects, an innovative work of considerable artistic merit. With its vividly intimate portrayal of a mind in the last stages of decay, and in its faithful attention to clinical detail, it is comparable in style and purpose to Georg Büchner's *Lenz* and should be ranked among Klaus Mann's best short works. It is something of a mystery why the author failed to recognize the potential in this kind of pure realism and did not seek to exploit it further, but, instead, returned once more to the politically-oriented descriptive prose which characterizes much of his fiction of the 1930's.

VII   Der Vulkan

Der Vulkan (The Volcano) is Klaus Mann's last and most ambitious published work of fiction. Although it may not be considered his best work, it is the one which the author himself admits cost him the greatest amount of time and effort and at the same time offered him a comparative degree of satisfaction. Yet with all the elation which comes from the accomplishment of such a long and difficult task, he injects an element of doubt into his reflections over the meaning of the work when he uses the words of its own character, Martin Korella, to describe his own inner thoughts about the fundamental reasons for being a writer:

For whom do I write? Poets have always reflected uneasily about this. And if they didn't know at all they claimed—haughtily and with resignation, proudly and desperately—:We are writing for those still to come! Not to you, the contemporaries, does our word belong; it belongs to the future, to the generations yet unborn.

Oh, what does one know about those still to come? What will their games, their cares be? How strange are they to us! We do not know what they love, what they will hate. Yet, it is they, to whom we must turn.... (*Wendepunkt*, p. 375)

These reflections seem to require two remarks: first, the notion that a writer writes for the benefit of future generations, even to the exclusion of the present one, is not necessarily shared by all writers and should be considered peculiar to Klaus Mann's personal philosophy; second, there is a sense of doubt that even future generations will find meaning in what the writer has to say today. Although these thoughts are those of a fictional character, the context in which they occur indicates that they are close to the true feelings of the author himself. The passage not only evidences the beginnings of a sense of uncertainty about the meaning of his function as a writer, it also demonstrates the continuing close sense of identification which he had with many of the principal characters in his work. Martin Korella is another fictional representation of Klaus Mann.

Der Vulkan, like its early predecessor, *Treffpunkt im Unendlichen*, is a compendium of loosely connected concurrent episodes about a host of characters who are only remotely related to one another by their actions, but share a common social and historical milieu, conditioned in this case by their exile. It is what Fritz Strich has aptly termed a *Roman des Nebeneinander* (novel of side-by-side).[17] Klaus Mann gives a brief but concise description of the novel's contents when he enumerates the multifarious problems and preoccupations of its characters:

The remembered and the surmised, dream and thought, insight and feeling, the death instinct, sensuality and the struggle (struggle, physical power, murder, and sacrifice as the paradoxically desperate consequence of moral decision), music and dialectics, the neurosis of uprootedness, homesickness as hostage and stimulant, befriended faces and beloved voices, landscapes of my life (Paris, Prague, Zurich, Amsterdam, the Engadin, New York, the Island of Mallorca, Vienna, the Côte d'Azure), the grimace of infamy, the glory of pity, (why no angels, since there are devils?), many forms of flight, of *escapism* (deadly balsam of the opiate! ecstasy and torment of the disease!), many forms of heroism (Spain! And didn't one also know of examples of heroism in the Third Reich?), encounters, farewells, anxieties, loneliness, embrace and conception, the birth of a child, and again struggle and again farewell, again loneliness, the pathos of the "in vain," the decision for the "in spite of." (*Der Vulkan*, p. 374)

Almost all of the various motifs mentioned here have occurred, in one guise or another, in Klaus Mann's earlier works. Rather than striking out in completely new directions, it would seem that in his new novel, Klaus Mann was attempting to reiterate and consolidate many of the problems which had concerned him previously, in a final *opus* of far-reaching dimensions. The familiar themes of "escapism," duty versus inclination, homosexuality and death, and others are once again woven into a narrative tapestry which draws much of its material from the author's experiences of the recent and distant past.

The central character, Martin Korella, who bears the strongest autobiographical traits of all the characters in the novel, is a frustrated writer who commits gradual suicide in a prolonged losing battle against morphine addiction. Although here is the first extensive treatment of this particular problem in Klaus Mann's work, there are lesser manifestations of it in the earlier works. It is the principal theme of the very early story, *Heinrich Hollmann, Geschichte einer Jugend*, which exists now only in summary form in *Kind dieser Zeit*. It is also the prime characteristic of Froschele, one of the more lamentable secondary characters of *Treffpunkt im Unendlichen*. Of greatest significance for the autobiographical character of the work is the fact that Klaus himself became addicted to morphine before he wrote *Der Vulkan* and remained addicted to it periodically for the remainder of his career.[18]

Martin Korella is the last in a long series of "young European intellectuals" in Klaus Mann's published work, who despairs of his writing abilities and falls victim to a strong death-impulse in the form of narcotics addiction. It is his ambition, never fulfilled, to write a monumental novel about the problems of the emigration from a first-hand viewpoint, which will stand as a document of the trials of his generation, for the benefit of future generations. Upon his death, Martin's mission falls to Kikjou, his homosexual lover, who also proves himself unable to accomplish the task.

The second major plot sequence, almost totally unrelated to the first, involves Marion von Kammer, another character clearly modelled after Erika Mann, who, after her exile from Germany, finds the opportunity to continue her political activity in the United States. Benjamin Abel, the middle-aged professor, also finds his way to America, where he forms what appears to be a stable relationship with Marion. A baby, which is conceived as a result of Marion's indiscretion with a young Italian and selflessly accepted by Abel in demonstration of his devotion, becomes a symbol of continuity, a promise that their efforts may be perpetuated in succeeding generations. The situation here is similar to that in *Kindernovelle*, where an inauspicious birth provides the protagonist with some incentive to continue in what would otherwise be an almost intolerable existence. The relationship between Abel and Marion, as tenuous as it appears to be, is one of the rare instances in the works of Klaus Mann where a man and woman have managed to find a lasting *modus vivendi* and a certain measure of happiness. Professor Abel is also one of the few significant characters in the novel who are not youthful.

As in earlier novels of the emigration, Klaus Mann has created a host of secondary characters who are thoughtfully constructed and contribute significantly to the general theme of exile. Such a character is Marion's sister, Tilly, who, caught up in a massive internal conflict between her loyalty to her exiled lover—who is being pursued by Nazi agents in another part of Europe—and her guilt over the unwanted child of another man growing in her body, commits suicide. Johanna, in *Flucht in den Norden*, could easily have shared a similar fate had she not made the crucial decision to cast her lot with those who were actively fighting Fascism. An industrialist named Bernheim, who bears a resemblance to the philanthropic W. B. Beyer in *Treffpunkt im Unendlichen*, is brutally treated by the Nazis as a result of his decision to move to Austria.

Another significant secondary character, consciously modelled after a close acquaintance of Klaus Mann, is Marcel Poiret, a second fictional representation of René Crevel, the young French poet who had provided the inspiration for the character of Till in *Kindernovelle*. Marcel represents the last in a long line of Klaus Mann characters who find temporary solutions to their problems by engaging in political action. His decision to participate in the Spanish Civil War parallels Klaus and Erika's own involvement in the conflict, when they visited Spain in 1938 as observers. Marcel dies as a result of his opposition to Fascism; but his death, in contrast to that of Martin Korella, occurs in pursuit of a noble cause. It is as though Klaus Mann, through his portrayal of Marcel's heroic death, tried to revive the memory of René Crevel, whose suicide had occurred several years earlier; in so doing, he was able to salvage an image of his departed friend by giving symbolic meaning to his otherwise senseless death. The child which is born to Marion and Abel is named Marcel, in honor of Marion's former husband, and stands as a symbol of renewal, a hope that what could not be accomplished in their time would some day indeed be realized.

In contrast to both Martin and Marcel stands David Deutsch, the only academic intellectual in the novel, and the one in whom perhaps the greatest hope of stability and future accomplishment lies. His ambition is to write a sociological study of the emigration, and, although he, too, is despondent about the ultimate value of his undertaking, he is able to achieve a measure of serenity and detachment which the other two lack. Where Martin and Marcel are opposite manifestations of essentially the same emotional conflict, David manages to find a middle ground in his emotional response to the rigors of exile. He is also the only one of the three who survives.

The most puzzling and, at the same time, perhaps most fascinating in this motley array of characters is Kikjou, the puerile transvestite who is Martin Korella's constant companion and lover. In a sense, Kikjou may be the novel's most important character, for it is on him that the long, symbolic final scene is centered. He has taken upon himself the mission of completing Martin Korella's great unfinished novel of emigration, "the precise chronicle of our confusions, sufferings, and also our hopes," which, as it becomes rapidly clear, he is incapable of fulfilling. The final scene, which bears some stylistic similarity to the work of Thomas Mann, presents another of Klaus Mann's final expressions of strained optimism, containing the hope that the problems of his youthful protagonists will one day be solved. There is a strong sense of irony in the portrayal of Klaus's frailest, most helpless character attempting in vain to complete a task which the author himself has just completed without undue self-sacrifice. The irony of the final scene, however, contrasts sharply with the earnestness of the novel as a whole. Beneath the work lies an undercurrent of desperation, a plea for the recognition of a lost, uprooted generation, for which the author considered himself a primary spokesman and felt an almost mystical sense of responsibility.

An additional attribute of the final scene is the appearance of a symbol which has by now become familiar in the endings of Klaus Mann's novels, the angel. As in two relatively early works, *Der fromme Tanz* and *Alexander*, the angel functions as a divine intervener, a kind of *deus ex machina*, who attempts to mediate between the respective protagonists' conflicting emotions and at the same time injects an element of reality into their passionate and somewhat distorted self-appraisals. In contrast to the angel of *Alexander*, whose hands are wounded and who weeps over his hero's desperate revelations, the angel of *Der Vulkan*, with his bowler hat and threadbare suit assumes a jaunty, Chaplinesque pose: Martin Gregor-Dellin writes, "It is the same angel as in André Gide's 'Counterfeiters,' temperate in his instructions, ironically to the point in his speech and therefore still stranger than the angel of the Alexander novel, who raged, sparkled, and wept."[19] The angel takes Kikjou on a whirlwind tour of the Earth, where he witnesses the activities of the remaining characters in the novel: Benjamin and Marion Abel, who have made a home for themselves in the United States; David Deutsch in Paris; Hans Schütte, who has managed to survive the fighting in the Spanish Civil War and plans to continue the struggle against Fascism on another front; and, finally, Dieter, an anonymous deserter from the German army, who attempts to escape to freedom by crossing a treacherous glacier near the Swiss border. The final pages contain some words of hope—and admonition—a mandate from God Himself, in the same ironic tone:

The driven-about, homeless, everywhere alien one has a comparatively good chance of becoming true to the almighty plan. You should be courageous; because the fatherly conception of your fulfillment, the Divine Will to utopia, is not only very sensible, but also audacious! The life which you could put on the line is not such a big thing. With a sword you were driven out of paradise; with a sword you should win it back. You must fight for the homeland, you homeless ones!'' (*Vulkan*, p. 416)

The call to arms presented here is not advanced merely as a means of fighting Fascism and regaining the lost homeland. It is at the same time a utopian charter, a rallying cry around which a new society will be built out of the ruins of the old, and the millennium will finally arrive. The sentiments expressed here are very similar to those voiced by Klaus Mann's Alexander, in the presence of a similar heavenly messenger, but under completely different circumstances. What Alexander failed to accomplish through the power of the sword Klaus Mann saw as a realistic possibility in his own time. The trials and sacrifices of the emigration were a prelude—indeed, almost a precondition—to the establishment of "the kingdom of happiness on Earth." It is no coincidence that, after the onset of the war which Klaus predicted with such apodictic certainty as many as five years earlier, he followed the mandate expressed by the characters in his own novels and decided to take an active part in the world-wide struggle against the desecrators of his homeland.

CHAPTER 5

The Last Decade: A Prelude to the Apocalypse

I The Beginning of the Second World War

ALTHOUGH the quantity of Klaus Mann's published works written after 1939 is relatively small in comparison to his output of the previous decade, there is every indication that the intensity with which he worked and the amount of written material he produced did not abate, even toward the very end of his life. The number of unpublished works now located in the Klaus Mann Archive in Munich which were written during the 1940's is at least as great as that of all the known works, both published and unpublished, which bear earlier dates. One probable reason for the diminution in his publishing capability is the simple fact that, with the onset of war, a large portion of his potential readership on the Continent was abruptly cut off, and the Querido Verlag, on which he had relied so heavily for the publication of his writings during exile was no longer operable. And, although he had written a pair of non-fiction books in English dealing with the problems of exile (*Escape to Life,* 1939; *The Other Germany*, 1940), he had not succeeded in attracting a sufficiently large English-speaking audience to warrant significant support from an American publisher. In a decision which was prompted by practical as well as emotional considerations, Klaus Mann resolved to renounce his mother tongue in his writing and, thenceforth, to produce original works only in English. It was a promise which he was to keep almost to the end of his life.

The chapters in *Der Wendepunkt* which describe the years 1940-1945 are written in the form of a diary. The entry for September 24, 1940, reads as follows: "The novella *Speed* completed, my first narrative attempt in the new language. Not satisfied. The epic style seems incomparably more difficult to strike than the critical-interpretive or the journalistic-reporting." (*Wendepunkt*, p. 408) The work mentioned here, which was never published, contains numerous irregularities in style and usage, characteristic of a German writer who has not yet completely mastered all the intricacies of idiomatic English. Nevertheless, the story contains some distinct elements of characterization typical of Klaus Mann's earlier style, along with some aspects not seen before, which can probably be attributed to his recently acquired and unique view of American culture.

Speed is the story of an Austrian expatriate named Karl Kroll who has fallen on difficult times because his wife, on learning of his Jewish background, has divorced him. He lives in New York at the home of a married couple named Prokoff, and it is there that he meets the young man named "Speed" and forms a rather bizarre attachment to him. As the story progresses, it becomes clear that Speed's motives have been less than honest and that he has intended all along to abuse the relationship with the older man. He introduces Kroll to marijuana, only to involve him in a grotesque scheme to extort money. Speed and his friend Jim, returning battered and bloody from an impromptu brawl, attempt to convince Kroll that Speed has been arrested on charges of possession of narcotics. They demand money, ostensibly in order to bribe the magistrate presiding over Speed's trial, then threaten to expose Kroll in the event of his refusal to turn over the money as the "pusher" who introduced them to narcotics in the first place. Kroll, in a quandary at first, becomes convinced of Speed's duplicity on witnessing his making love to Mrs. Prokoff and decides to break off all further relations with the wayward youth. The end of the novella finds Kroll stronger and wiser for his experience, with a renewed determination to make a better life for himself in his new homeland.

The by now familiar theme of the uprooted political emigré is here combined with the equally familiar one of the drifting, homeless youth, without clearly defined goals or aspirations. Speed is still another figure in the long line of unattached, wayward Kaspar Hauser types whose clearest expressions can be found in the characters of Erik, Till, and Niels. What the story surprisingly lacks is any significant political motivation, up to now present in all of Klaus Mann's works dealing with emigration and exile. With the exception of a brief reference to the Jewish origin of the main character, the story contains no political references whatsoever. The theme of narcotics addiction, with which the author had previously dealt, here assumes a peculiarly "American" cast. What in earlier works is associated with the morbid regression or downfall of the main characters becomes the relatively innocuous vehicle of an abortive intrigue, which leaves the participants unharmed and even in a somewhat better state than before. It is likely that the author's familiarity with the American drug culture, which had been established in New York long before he arrived, extended at least to the relatively harmless and less debilitating aspects of this highly controversial facet of American social life.

A story written in a similar narrative style, but with a totally different outcome, is "Three Star Hennessy," also completed in 1940. The plot in this instance centers on a heroine, Catherine, who is visiting the United States after a sojourn in France, where her husband, a French flier, has recently been killed in battle against the Nazis. She is accompanied by her matronly Aunt Jane, who is aware of her niece's unstable emotional state and wishes to make her stay in America as recuperative as possible. They visit a small out-of-the-way restaurant in New York City, where Catherine orders a bottle of Hennessy cognac and proceeds to get uninhibitedly drunk. As she becomes more intoxicated, she begins to unleash the long pent-up feelings of hostility and despair which threaten to consume her. In a last outburst of tragic exhibitionism, she begins to enthrall the crowd which has gathered around her to witness the impending disintegration of her character: "Catherine—an irresistable maenad—conducted and enchanted the crowd. She was alarmingly beautiful—transfigured in a sort of wild and aggressive trance. I looked at her, with delight and apprehension. What a disquieting goddess of intoxication!—the white flame of her face, crowned by the slanting helmet; the fumbling grandeur of her gestures; splendor and misery of her meager body. Her mouth was wide open—a black hole in a tragic mask."[1]

The character of Catherine bears great resemblance to that of Suzanne Cobière, whom Klaus Mann conceived more than ten years before. Possessed of the same "hysteria" as her predecessor, Catherine meets a similar orgiastic fate, which is born out of a unique combination of exultation, sexual release, and despair. She is still another representative of that type of Klaus Mann character whose resolution to the massive conflict which threatens to engulf her is one of cataclysmic, self-destructive excess.

The story contains an additional element, rarely seen in earlier Klaus Mann works, a sympathetic and therefore less than objective observer, who provides it with a narrative frame. His sympathy with the heroine extends to the point of his feeling anxiety over his inability to come to her aid in the crisis: "Catherine's outcry—raucous and triumphant—soared beyond the chaotic noise. But now her voice faltered. I noticed, with painful surprise, that the shining pallor of her face could turn even more colorless. She staggered: in a moment or two she would fall. I felt that I ought to prop her up, to protect her, to call for a doctor, the police; to do something. . . ." (Klaus Mann Archive).

A similar narrative frame can be found in the story, "Le Dernier Cri," which was published in the popular magazine, *Esquire*, in May, 1941. While the main character does not fit the established pattern of youth in conflict, which has shown itself to be a dominant theme in Klaus Mann's work—she is an old woman—she nevertheless exhibits some of the more salient features of his typical youthful characters. The story takes place in a somewhat decrepit hotel, situated in a once fashionable Austrian town which has seen better days. The narrator, possessed of the same combination of sympathy and morbid curiosity as his counterpart in "Three Star Hennessy," becomes intrigued with the personality of one of the few permanent residents of the hotel, the Baroness de la Motte-Tribolière, the last of the great courtesans, an ancient but still proud remnant of a bygone era. The story takes on a grotesque air as the grand old lady acts out her bizarre charade of past glories in an atmosphere which is at once vacuous and decadent. Although it is again for the most part bereft of the political commentary which pervades a good deal of Klaus Mann's fiction of the previous decade, the story contains an occasional sampling of the author's gloomy appraisal of the situation which exists outside the consciously artificial atmosphere of the old hotel:

A world convulsed by the fever of permanent crisis has no room or time for the luxurious whims of individuals. These are bad days, indeed, for the *ars amandi*. A new militant pathos, noisy, crude, and relentless, sweeps away the sins and charms of a more settled society. A new perfunctory libertinism depreciates the traditional rites and subtle circumstances of costly vices: the odd morality of 1940 has no objection to the bombing of open cities, but disapproves strictly of sensual refinements that might be pernicious to the national strength. The rich finance political parties instead of expensive women; the poor get intoxicated by the thudding eloquence of dictators; tyrants turn ascetic—youngsters murderous—and the Baroness de La Motte Tribolière spends her days in gloomy loneliness—musing about the cruel change of all worldly things . . .[2]

A more controlled and subdued form of the despair which characterizes the fates of both Suzanne Cobière and Catherine exists here as well, although it is combined with a strong sense of irony and nostalgia which is absent from the others:

"We are doomed—all of us. You and I, and all these lusty men and women. The flowers, the champagne, the beautiful girls; artists, courtesans, princes, adventurers, and poets—doomed . . ." "Dernier Cri!" she whimpers again and again, convulsed with laughter and agony. "You are right, my friend! Oh, how right you are! Our last scream—here it is! *I* am the last scream—the last sign—the last grin of an epoch . . . *Le dernier cri*, c'est moi . . ."[3]

Behind the heavy irony and the fascination with the grotesque which the story is intended to display lies a more profound and potentially disturbing sentiment which must be attributed to Klaus Mann's personal view of the world, a reflection of a private mood only partially masked by his artistic fantasy. In previous works we have seen a number of characters, endowed to a greater or lesser extent with traits or peculiarities which have some bearing on the author's day-to-day experience at some particular time in his life. In this instance, we are presented with a character, produced wholly out of the author's creative imagination, with no known resemblance to persons of his acquaintance, but who expresses thoughts reflecting Klaus Mann's deepening pessimism over the world political situation, which was now beginning to affect his emotional as well as his intellectual life.

II   Decision

On the first of November, 1940, as Klaus began writing his first notes for "Le Dernier Cri," he had already been investigating the possibility of publishing a second literary journal in exile which was to have a similar format and philosophy as the short-lived *Sammlung*. Immediately following a paragraph in *Der Wendepunkt* in which he makes brief mention of his work on the story, there is the following cursory reference to his mood at the time: "In between, hours of terrible sadness. Will they become more frequent? The death wish. Icy consolation of nothingness" (*Wendepunkt*, p. 411). Apparently, the anticipation of his new undertaking and the large investment in time and effort which the preparations for the journal, named *Decision*, entailed enabled Klaus, at least for a time, to stave off the effects of what appears to be the onset of a profound and serious depression.

Like *Die Sammlung, Decision* was intended to be a journal dedicated to literary criticism and political commentary. In an introductory section to the first issue, which appeared in January, 1941, Klaus outlined the basic purpose of the journal and briefly explained its philosophy: "Social programs, the tenets of philosophy, ethics and esthetics, the moral import of history, the implications of scientific developments, the aims and the practice of pedagogy—all these must be re-analyzed and tested in the light of recent events. And, above all, the unquenchable flame of creative writing must be permitted to burn on. Young story-tellers want to mirror and clarify the conditions of our life. The mysterious solace and lament of poetry remain indispensable—now as a thousand years ago."[4] Like *Die Sammlung, Decision* solicited articles from a number of European writers in exile, as well as from contemporary American intellectuals of note. On its board of editorial advisors were Stefan Zweig, Sherwood Anderson, W. H. Auden, Edward Benes, Julien Green, Vincent Sheean, and Robert E. Sherwood, among others. Thomas Mann also made an active contribution.

Almost from the beginning, the journal suffered from financial difficulties. Since it was apparent that *Decision* would attract a limited clientele and would be unlikely to sustain itself on the revenue from subscriptions alone, Klaus made a concerted effort to solicit funds from other sources, primarily wealthy benefactors. One of these, a Mr. A. A. Strelsin, offered to help raise twenty thousand dollars for the journal on the condition that Thomas Mann be named Chief Editor, a stipulation which was both impracticable for Thomas Mann and demeaning to his son, who bore almost the total responsibility for the creation of the enterprise and did most of the work to maintain it. After an attempt at a compromise in which

Thomas Mann would agree to become a regular contributor and would be named as an "Editorial Advisor," the offer failed to materialize. Klaus did receive smaller contributions from Max Ascoli, a professor at the New School for Social Research in New York, and from Marshall Field, the department store magnate and publisher.

Despite Klaus's best efforts, the financial health of the journal continued to deteriorate through its first year of publication, so that in its second year, 1942, it began to be published bi-monthly, instead of monthly. It is clear from his letters that Klaus was deeply disturbed over the declining fortunes of his periodical, although he did his best to appear outwardly cheerful: "I am *terribly* sad. Not only, or not even above all, because of the loss of the journal itself or because of all the fruitless effort and toil, but because the whole mess looms right before my eyes, no matter how little one wants, needs, and appreciates the likes of us in this questionable world. It is the many *small* blows and pinpricks that actually bother me more than the fiasco 'as such' ".[5] What troubled Klaus more than the prospect of *Decision's* imminent demise and the immense amounts of time and energy which he had invested in order to keep the ailing journal going was the fact that he was not receiving the recognition for his effort which he so richly deserved; in some instances, his position as Editor-in-Chief was not even acknowledged:

Today there came from the Librarian of Congress a very nice letter addressed to—Miss Rukeyser [Muriel Rukeyser, Associate Editor], in which he thanks her cordially for her "deeply moving offer," appreciates everything, and concludes with a warmly formulated wish for the periodical: "I am certain that the experience and the very great talents of *the group of writers who have created 'Decision'* (!!) will find tremendous scope in the months ahead, and I hope very much you will find some means to keep the magazine itself going." My name doesn't appear in the whole thing. Our telegram was naturally signed with both names; moreover, the librarian knows only too well that the whole thing was my creation and affair: I had a conference with him even before the first issue came out. Non-citizens are not honored with answers from American patriots.[6]

Klaus seems to blame the failure of others to grant him proper recognition on the premise that he was being discriminated against because of his foreign background. Perhaps in the back of his mind lay the suspicion, never voiced, that he was a victim of the anti-German sentiment which was prevalent, even among intellectuals, shortly before America's entry into the Second World War. No matter what his private thoughts may have been, he was doubtless acutely aware that the attention and interest which the name of Thomas Mann evoked among Americans did not automatically carry over to the mention of his son.

Klaus Mann had little real justification for his despondency over the eventual discontinuance of his second literary journal. During its brief lifetime of little more than a year, *Decision* printed a wide variety of literary and political essays and short works of fiction and poems by distinguished American and European writers, all of whom willingly lent their support to an enterprise whose value they recognized and cherished. Try as he might, Klaus was never able to dispel the impression which had been created in the public mind that *Decision* was just another periodical created to foster solidarity among exiled European intellectuals, a "refugee review." Its predecessor, *Die Sammlung*, had succumbed to political pressures and reactionary forces, both within and without; *Decision*, subtitled "a review of free culture," whose political stance Klaus Mann made no attempt to conceal, succumbed largely to public apathy.

III   The Turning Point

In July, 1941, after the first few issues of *Decision* had gone to press and preparations were being made for subsequent ones, Klaus Mann made up his mind to begin work on still another book, a second autobiography, to be named *The Turning Point*. He chose to write an autobiography in preference to another novel: "Can a novel be completely serious, completely sincere? Perhaps. But I do not want to write one; not now, not at this hour. I am tired of all literary clichés and tricks. I am tired of all masks, all hypocrisy. Is it art itself that I am tired of? I don't want to play any more. I want to confess." (*Wendepunkt*, p. 422) These sentiments echo those of Martin Korella, who had also reached a point where he despaired of writing fiction and aspired instead to creating a work which would exert a lasting guiding influence over his generation, a work which he never completed.

When viewed in its entirety, *The Turning Point* is not a true confession. It is written in the chatty, informative style which characterizes many of the previous personal narratives, *Kind dieser Zeit* in particular, from which it draws much of the material for its early chapters. It is a lighthearted, sensitive account of a great variety of the author's experiences from his early childhood up to June, 1942, when the book was completed. It expresses his opinions on an entire range of subjects, from politics to art, and describes his relations with a host of significant personalities—some of whom he knew intimately, others whom he met only in passing. Thomas Mann, after reading the book for the first time, remarked, "Was it, as the story of one's life, a somewhat premature undertaking? One will perhaps say so, but if you had waited until the age of fifty, the early memories, which in confessions are always the best, would no longer have been able to acquire the freshness and comic gaiety which they have here."[7] Despite its charm and engaging style, however, *The Turning Point* lacks the depth of insight into the author's own personality which would qualify it as a truely analytical autobiography.

The attack on Pearl Harbor on December 7, 1941, brought about a sudden and profound change in the direction of Klaus Mann's life, with implications so far-reaching that Klaus himself could not have had an inkling of all of them. By the end of January, it was becoming clear that *Decision* was rapidly approaching bankruptcy and that the January-February issue would be the last. At the end of May, he finished the last chapter of *The Turning Point* and commenced writing a long-planned biographical study of André Gide, which he was able to publish in New York with the help of his old friend and publisher, Fritz Landshoff. In the meantime, he had been corresponding with his draft board in the hope of changing his military classification so that he could enlist in the American army. His diary entry for October 24, 1942, contains one of a series of expressions of the suicidal moods which were to occur with increasing frequency during the latter half of the last decade of his life; the short statement which he purports to have uttered almost a year earlier is repeated here several times, like a leitmotiv: "Terrible sadness—overshadowing everything. The death wish." (*Wendepunkt*, p. 436)

On December 14, Klaus underwent the last of several physical examinations to determine his fitness for military service. The results were positive, and within two weeks he was a soldier in the United States Army. His fiction written during and immediately after the war contains few references, either direct or indirect, to his own experiences as a soldier. The single exception to this rule is an unpublished short story, "The Monk," written some time during 1943. It takes place in an army training camp at an unspecified location in the United States, where an older recruit, nicknamed "the Monk," because of his celibate disposition and general aloofness, is being harassed by the younger, more worldly men in his company. Although his origins are obscure, it becomes apparent that he is an intellectual, in sharp contrast to his companions, and that he possesses certain artistic gifts, which only serve to widen the emotional and spiritual gap which exists between himself and his fellow soldiers. He also proves to be physically inept, and his inability to master the procedures of basic training brings down upon him the disapproval of his superiors as well. The grotesque climax of the story occurs when, one night while on guard duty he is confronted by an obscenely drunken prostitute who has erroneously wandered into camp and unceremoniously attached herself to the hapless soldier. In a quandary over how best to discharge his duty while at the same time maintaining his accustomed sense of decorum, he enters the barracks with his bizarre charge tenaciously clinging to him. His comrades, who greet him with a mixture of surprise and admiration, refuse to believe that he has not deliberately accosted the woman for his own pleasure, and, despite his efforts to convince them of the contrary, they instantly grant him the approval and sense of belonging which has been absent in their relationship until then. In the end, after they persuade him to cut out a silhouette depicting the imagined sexual embrace, he produces a strange image of a man and woman facing each other, devoid of any sexual connotation, with the symbol of a cross set between them. The true nature of the Monk's moral and sexual identity remains as mysterious as ever.

"The Monk" presents us with an almost classical portrayal of the *Aussenseiter* (outsider), similar in many respects to the grotesque characters in the early stories of Thomas Mann, and once again endowed with certain autobiographical characteristics. The "monk" is approximately thirty-five, a year less than Klaus when he entered the army. His speech is tinged with a slight foreign accent of indefinable origin. Although in his autobiographies Klaus reveals little about his relations with his fellow soldiers, it is likely that their attitude toward a recruit some ten years their senior, who spoke with a german accent, resembled that of the soldiers in the story.

The story's ambiguous ending parallels the endings of earlier Klaus Mann works, where the respective heroes' failure to find fulfillment is a rule rather than an exception. The final description of the Monk's relationship with the prostitute gives further evidence of the author's peculiar view of the ultimate relationship between the sexes:

They saw two human figures—a woman and a man—neatly profiled against a white background. They did not stand close together but were separated from each other by a cross and a gap which looked like an open grave. The woman was young and proud and very beautiful. There was a faint glory around her head—a halo of youth and innocence, as it were. The man—gaunt and stooping—wore a foot-long mantle and a big slouch hat, which gave him the appearance of an old, romantic wanderer—a beggar, a sorcerer, or a priest. But, curiously, it was the woman whose gesture seemed sacerdotal. The wide motion of her spread arms did not suggest embrace and tenderness (and, anyhow, she could not have reached the man, over the cross and the grave). This generous salute meant something else—a blessing, a benediction, enthusiastically presented to the humble pilgrim. (K.M. Archive)

The mutual unapproachability of the man and the woman is accompanied by the religious symbolism which is also characteristic of the endings of other Klaus Mann works. Once again, the act of love, which this distorted and ritualized scene is meant to represent, is associated with the symbolism of death. The man, who is cast in the image of an older, more experienced, but evidently none-the-wiser Kaspar Hauser, is blessed by a woman who resembles the Madonna in the dream sequence which marks the beginning and end of *Der fromme Tanz*. Heterosexual love, along with the Monk's still undetermined origin and destiny, remain eternally shrouded in mystery.

Klaus spent 1943 in a succession of military camps in the United States, where he received the training necessary for active duty overseas. He must have impressed his superiors with his intelligence and determination to take part in the war effort, because he was promoted directly from Private First Class to Staff Sergeant within four months of his enlistment. Because of his superior intellect and his fluency in German, he was assigned to the Psychological Warfare Branch of Military Intelligence, the propaganda arm of the American armed forces. After a brief sojourn in North Africa, his unit was assigned to the Italian campaign, where Klaus was engaged primarily in composing propaganda leaflets and appearing at the front with a loudspeaker, urging the Germans to surrender. He was frequently under enemy fire and risked his life on more than one occasion.

When the war ended, Klaus remained in uniform and became a staff writer for the American military journal *Stars and Stripes*, where he wrote numerous articles, primarily political. One such article, entitled "Are All Germans Nazis?", is a continuation of his attempt to exonerate a portion of the German people who opposed Hitler, which he had begun in his book, *The Other Germany,* before the war. In contrast, the descriptions of his encounters with such notables as Emil Jannings and Richard Strauss express the harshest disdain for men of stature who had remained in Germany during the Nazi period and had made some form of accommodation with Hitler and his ideology. For the first time in over a decade, Klaus was able to travel freely over the shattered landscape which had once been his homeland and concern himself once more with the question of what was to become of the country whose problems had occupied his mind for so long. Once again, his approach to the political problems of a Europe to which he had been devoted and at the same time denied access for so many years takes the form of a troubled question, which reveals a sense of urgency which had not been present in the self-assured, rhetorical questions in the writings of his youth: "*How do we want Germany*? Is there even a program according to which the beaten, shattered *Reich* may be rebuilt, physically and morally renewed? Sometimes, in fact, it seems as if such a plan simply *did not exist*. What explanation would there be for the contradictory, peevishly paradoxical character of our politics?" (*Wendepunkt*, p. 498)

That Klaus intended to deal at length with the political problems of post-war Germany is revealed in a brief proposal found among his posthumous papers, entitled "A Book on Postwar Germany," along with an accompanying letter to an editor of Creative Age Press, which had published his biography of André Gide two years earlier. The letter, dated October 20, 1945, contains an outline of the proposed book and requests an advance of one thousand dollars, which was evidently not granted. The book was intended to present a survey of Klaus's impressions of the social and political situation in post-war Germany and was to contain his thoughts as expressed by a semi-fictional observer, similar to the "neutral," who gives a summary of the author's views in the concluding chapter of *The Other Germany*:[8]

A German-born European who has become an American and a citizen of the world returns to his old continent and old country as an American soldier: this strange, indeed, adventurous situation will be the main theme, the emotional leitmotiv of my story. Yet I do not intend to limit the scope of my interests and observations to this highly personal, somewhat nostalgic approach. By describing my own experiences and reactions in Germany, I hope also to clarify some problems of general significance. (K. M. Archive)

Although the book was never written, the questions raised by Klaus's intention to write it contain echoes of past concerns, as well as doubts about the future:

Do the German people realize their responsibility? Do they repent their guilt? Are there any signs indicative of a moral and political awakening? What will be Germany's future place and function within the family of European nations? What kind of role may the country be destined to play in the future drama of mankind? Do the Germans tend toward Communism? Will the Reich be dominated by the Russians? Is it to become the battlefield of World War Three? What is America's stake in Germany? What should be the American policy in Central Europe? Does the German nation still command reserves of moral and intellectual energies, or is it altogether exhausted, corrupt, depleted of creative forces? Is there any hope that a Federation of European States, or the United States of Europe, may eventually come into being? (K. M. Archive)

The final question is an indication that the Pan-Europeanism of the author's youth was still very much alive in his post-war idealism.

Two works of fiction, both fragments stemming from the early post-war period, are "House Hollberg" and "Fräulein." The former, a dramatic sketch, which could have been intended as a radio play, is based on the author's return to the Mann's old house on Poschingerstrasse in Munich in May, 1945. It concerns an American soldier of German descent who returns to the ruins of his family home in Munich and encounters a female war correspondent in search of a story. They find an old, half-blind woman in the ruins, who reveals herself to be Else, the former maid of the Hollberg family. She relates a complicated story of events which occurred in the house after the family, headed by a liberal anti-Fascist professor, fled to Switzerland in 1933. The house had been made into a *Lebensborn*, an institution for the breeding of racially pure children, administered by the *S.S.* This element is based on a real event, which Klaus learned of in his encounter with a young woman who was living in the ruins of the real Mann house near the end of the war. The sketch is laden with autobiographical references, some of which can be traced to the most distant, others to the more recent past.

"Fräulein," the outline of a novel, deals with the problems of a German girl, Lotte, who is caught in the Russian zone of occupation immediately after the war. She becomes involved with a pair of Russian soldiers, from one of whom she contracts syphilis, and is cured by Dr. David Dorn, a former Fascist, with whom she establishes a bizarre, but semi-permanent relationship. After her escape to the Western Sector, she has a succession of brief affairs with a number of men, each representing one of the major nationalities and political persuasions representative of post-war Berlin: British, French and American. She ultimately marries the American, Jim. Dr. Dorn is jubilant over the union, because it provides him with a means of infiltrating the American Sector and aiding the rebirth of his Neo-Nazi organization.

Lotte is a rare example of a Klaus Mann anti-heroine, the exact counterpart of Johanna, who also confuses her political with her sexual life. She is symbolic of Klaus Mann's view of the dual nature of the post-war German character, with its attractive potential for reconstruction and development on the one hand, and its destructive, regressive tendencies, on the other. Dr. Dorn, the embodiment of evil genius, is the post-war equivalent of Dr. Massis in *Treffpunkt im Unendlichen.*

Although the manuscript of the novel consists of several versions of the first chapter and a fragment of another, not enough on which to base a critical evaluation, the outline which is present marks the beginning of a trend in Klaus Mann's post-war fiction in which the historical polarity of East and West plays a major symbolic role. Analogous to the politically oriented works of Klaus's youth, where his primary concern was the essential difference between the American and European socio-political outlooks, here attention is centered primarily on the eastward shift of political power, of which Klaus had begun to become aware well before the end of the Second World War.

IV   The Seventh Angel

The end of *Der Wendepunkt* coincides with the end of the Second World War. Although, as Klaus points out in an afterword to the book, written a scant month before his death, it was not merely a German translation of *The Turning Point*, but a new, revised and extended version of his autobiography, he did not see fit to carry it through the post-war years. Consequently, all accounts of his activities from the end of 1945 until his death must rely on the personal recollections of friends and relatives and other secondary sources. His decision to end the work where he did may have been based on an intuition that the end of the war represented a turning point in his private life as well as in the course of contemporary history. The ideas expressed at the end of the work smack of a strong, deep-rooted ambivalence, the determined, apodictic response to a greater, more extreme crisis than the last; it is a response which contrasts with the more usual reactions of relief with which most of his contemporaries greeted the new era of peace:

The changes which come after the turning point may at first not seem very drastic, but will, in the course of time, become more drastic, from month to month, from year to year: in good times or bad. I prophesy that in 1965 we will have a world which will be very much worse than today's—or decidedly better. There is now only universal order or universal chaos, nothing in between. The *either-or*, to which Kierkegaard pledges us on a religious level—now it also confronts us in the socio-political sphere. We have reached the point from which only *one* step is possible: to general perdition or to general salvation.'' (*Wendepunkt*, p. 505)

Klaus was beginning to see himself in a dualistic world in which two opposing forces were perpetually at war with one another, threatening to engulf humanity as a whole. His role was beginning to shift from that of a spokesman for the youthful exiles struggling to regain their identity away from their lost homeland to that of post-war prophet of an impending worldwide cataclysm, the precise details of which he failed to specify.

The single work which stands out among all his planned writings of the post-war period and the only major work of fiction which he completed after 1945 is *Der siebente Engel* (The Seventh Angel), a play in three acts. It was written in Switzerland in 1946, in German, later revised and translated into English and French. The German version was distributed in manuscript form by the Europa Verlag, Zurich, which retained the German language rights to it. Unlike many other Klaus Mann works, which were conceived and written over a relatively short period of time, this one has a rather complicated history, consisting of several intermediary stages, each connected by the central theme of spiritualism. It was first conceived as a novel, to be entitled *Ghosts*, later transformed into a play, first called *The Deserters* and finally *The Dead Don't Care*. A letter included among the manuscripts indicates that Klaus attempted to have it published by Creative Age Press.

The Dead Don't Care is a complete play and bears many similarities to *The Seventh Angel*, but it has a different purpose. It is the story of a much-admired professor, James van Loyden, who has founded an organization devoted to spiritualism, which is located in his sumptuous residence, "Villa Pacific," on the coast of California. He is in the process of completing several books of a philosophical and pacifistic nature and requires the services of a medium, Alice McUlster, in order to communicate with his dead wife, Julia, to whom he was devoted in life and on whom he now relies heavily for inspiration and advice. The house is inhabited by a motley array of secondary characters, including Ted and Toy, a pair of precocious and problematic twins, and a hypochondriacal young woman named Marceline, who tries unsuccessfully to communicate with her husband Edward, who drowned when the ship he was travelling on was torpedoed by a German submarine. He drowned in an attempt to save the life of a sailor to whom Marceline, with a considerable feeling of guilt, later confesses an erotic attachment. The technique of mistaken identity is employed with the appearance of Johnny, the forerunner of the main character in *The Seventh Angel*, who immediately falls in love with Marceline. She notes a resemblance between Johnny and the sailor in whose attempted rescue Edward died, and she assumes that he has been sent as a substitute for her husband. The denouement, and probably the weakest point in the play, occurs when Alice McUlster and her accomplice, the Yogi Kadornath, another ill-conceived secondary character, reveal themselves to be agents of National Socialism, engaged in a conspiracy to defraud the professor by making him write pacifist-isolationist propaganda in the belief that he is carrying out the wishes of his departed wife.

As a whole, the play is badly organized and motivated. Written as it was during the war, it gives the impression of being a piece of popular anti-Nazi propaganda in the form of an intellectual surrealistic comedy. The result is a work which neither stimulates the imagination nor heightens the political consciousness of the reader. It does, however, contain the seeds of what was to become the much more carefully conceived, provocative, political-metaphysical tragicomedy, *The Seventh Angel*. Like its predecessor, *The Seventh Angel* takes place on an island off the coast of California, where the medium Vera Vanstraaten has taken control of the occult, quasi-political Vanstraaten Society, founded by her late husband, Jan. She has assumed the role of a priestess in order to carry out the work of her husband, who in life had been the propagator of a complex apocalyptic vision and in death is expected to communicate with his wife in order to indicate when the long-awaited end of the world is to occur. The vehicle for this pronouncement is a ritual in which the six Vanstraaten children, clothed as angels, await the advent of a seventh angel, whose trumpet will herald the cataclysm. The role of the seventh angel is reluctantly relegated to Jane, the oldest child and the shunned and feeble-minded offspring of an illegitimate union between the "Master" and a chambermaid. The cast of characters in the first act is completed by Judith Vanstraaten—invalid sister of the late Master, who provides the organizational leadership for the operation—and three professors, Uncle, Larue, and Li Tso, each representative of one of the three major World cultures, American, European and Oriental, respectively. Their only purpose in the undertaking is to see how they can profit financially from the impending disaster. Two minor characters, a cook and a governess, play small but significant roles.

Act One, Scene Two begins with an elaborately planned séance, during which Vera is finally to communicate with the Master. The expected communication does not occur, however; and in the Master's stead there appears a young sailor named Till, who has evidently come from the depths of the ocean and whom the participants of the séance assume to be a messenger from the Master, sent to reveal the final apocalyptic tidings. Till does not attempt to dispel their misapprehension and for a time pretends to be the expected messenger, until he develops strong erotic feelings for Vera and confesses that he is indeed mortal and had merely been out for a sail in his small boat when it was shipwrecked on the island. With considerable reluctance, Vera decides to take him as her lover. When Judith learns that Till has persuaded Vera of the inherent falseness of her calling and has invited her to leave the island with him, she becomes enraged over the prospect of the inevitable demise of her carefully built-up enterprise and begins to plot the unwelcome visitor's death. She tries to persuade the children to lead Till to an isolated, sacred part of the island, the *Andachtsklippe* (Contemplation Rock), and push him into the sea. Her plans are temporarily foiled when the children, won over by Till's charm and vitality, refuse to do her bidding. Jane, however, inadvertently assumes the task as she leads him to the cliff, where, apparently by accident, he falls to his death. Vera is distraught when the news of Till's death reaches her; but she is mollified when, in a séance later that evening, she is able to communicate with him from "the other side." He becomes the true mediator between the Master and his followers when he announces that the child which Vera carries as a result of their liaison is destined to become the long-awaited seventh angel. The conclusive implications of this revelation remain in doubt, for Vera's question as to whether the seventh angel is the herald of the apocalypse or the savior of the world goes unanswered. Vera, however, receives the news with optimism, as she announces her intention never to communicate with the other side again and decides to face a perilous world with joy and determination:

In darkness we all remain, as long as we must bear the dark torment and joy of earthly existence. It is also dark inside me, where life grows. But the fear is no longer there. The happiness which radiates from me—you would also find it if you no longer chose to seek it in foreign spheres. Do you still not know what mystery is to be plumbed here on Earth? Dare the inexpressible adventure which we call love—darkest affliction, most gleaming revelation! It is always worth it. All is well. Fear not.[9]

Superficially, Vera's final utterance would provide a fit ending for a modern morality play in which the potentially catastrophic ills of the world can be cured, or at least mitigated, by a return to reason and love. On a deeper level, however, the play is an allegory of the post-war world in crisis. If one considers it within the context of

Klaus Mann's previous creative endeavors from the earliest up to the most recent, it assumes a fitting place in a strikingly logical pattern. Klaus Mann had written plays before, although his last one had been published over fifteen years earlier. He had also attempted to create works of an allegorical-apocalyptic nature, which he never completed. Among his unpublished papers are some notes for a novel dating from 1937 and entitled *Nach der Sintflut* (After the Deluge). They depict the aftermath of a modern global cataclysm, in which Achilles and Penthesilea fight to the death in a world bereft of humanity. A fragment of a cantata entitled "Fluch und Segen" (Curse and Blessing), a dualistic representation of the myth of creation, which also reveals the author's messianic orientation, was written several years earlier.

What makes *The Seventh Angel* particularly noteworthy, both from a thematic and historical perspective, is the wealth of autobiographical material which it contains, some of it from the author's life contemporaneous with its writing, but most of it from the relatively distant past. Much of the characterization and plot material for the work can be traced directly to *Kindernovelle*. In approximate age and sex distribution the six children of the play correspond to the six Mann siblings.[10] The oldest girl, Ursula, fourteen, is one year older than the oldest boy, Kaspar, who bears the familiar autobiographical stamp. The members of the remaining two pairs of children, each consisting of one girl and one boy, are separated in age by a year, like their counterparts in the Mann family. The scene of action is moved from Bad Tölz to California, where the elder Manns had taken up residence when the play was written. The main character, Till, has the same name and character traits as his counterpart in *Kindernovelle*: "About 25, robust, handsome, intelligent; somewhat on the adventurous side: a young vagabond—slightly irresponsible, but full of dynamics, charm, imagination." (K. M. Archive)

An examination of the relations between the main characters offers considerable justification for comparison with *Kindernovelle*, as well as with other early works. Although Till matches his predecessor of some twenty years in character and temperament, his nautical origin brings to mind a character from another work of the same period, Erik, whose function in *Anja und Esther* is also that of the intruder, whose appearance has a profoundly liberating effect on the leading lady. Vera, whose origin and fate closely parallel

those of her predecessor, Christiane, differs in temperament from
the early heroine. Unlike Christiane, whose demeanor is generally
placid up to the point at which Till abandons her, Vera is, from the
start, high-strung, anxious and obsessed by her calling. As her love
affair with Till nears its climax, she is overcome with anxiety over
the knowledge of his true identity, and she begins to express
feelings of guilt associated with the thought of her infidelity toward
her late husband.

Vera's role as priestess gives the author still another opportunity
to associate the ultimate heterosexual fulfillment with death. At the
conclusion of the second act Vera articulates the fatal risk which
Till must take by expressing his love for her: "You cannot love me:
I am not human. My eyes have seen more than human eyes are permitted to see, my heart knows more than it is good for a human
heart to know; I am also in provinces in which no mortal should
tread. How could you love me? I am the beloved of the dead, death
is all around me, my embrace is deadly. . . ." (*Der siebente Engel*,
p. 62) The heroine of *Kindernovelle* is abandoned by her lover after
their child is conceived. The heroine of *The Seventh Angel* also
loses her lover, not by abandonment, but by death. Vera's personality is a unique mixture of passivity and maternal instinct, such as
that found in Marion of *Der Vulkan*—who also gives birth to a
child which lends hope to an otherwise moribund situation—and
the characteristic "hysteria," which is associated with such intensely disturbed female characters as Suzanne Cobière and, more
recently, Catherine of *Three Star Hennessy*. In all three instances
where a child is born, the event not only has a salutary effect on the
protagonists but also conveys a feeling that the course of events
which take place after the actual ends of the respective works will
eventually lead to a happy resolution.

The only character in the work who is difficult to classify is Jane,
one of the rare instances in Klaus Mann's fiction where a complete
outcast appears. Mentally retarded and shunned by children and
adults alike, she is finally doomed to live out her life in the company of a reclusive, demented old fisherman named Jakob. Like
the diminutive Kikjou of *Der Vulkan*, she suffers from a state of almost total ineffectuality, which makes her subservient to the whims
and good graces of those around her. Her inability to play the role
of the seventh angel is the symbolic trigger for the outcome of the

play. In the English version of the play, it is she, not Till, who falls to her death in the sea.

Although the basic plot structure of *Kindernovelle* is contained in *The Seventh Angel*, in the latter it has much greater allegorical significance. Whereas the former merely presents a psychological portrayal of a lonely woman who gains a sense of release by giving birth to the child of a nameless vagabond, the latter combines essentially the same components of the mystery of birth, or, in this instance, rebirth, to form a messianic allegory. The entire complex of events which lead up to the creation of the seventh angel has a deeply-rooted religious connotation as well as an affinity to the more recent concept of *Der Neue Mensch* (The New Man), which is an essential component in the ideology of German Expressionism. The various portrayals of angels which mark the endings of several earlier Klaus Mann works are here merged to form the apotheosis of his idealism in the crucial, final phase of his life. As has been noted, Klaus Mann abandoned almost entirely the experimental, ''Romantic'' style of his youthful works and wrote primarily politically-motivated, realistic prose during the 1930's. Although it may not be immediately apparent, the two basic structural levels of the play—the one a satirical representation of the conflict between the major world powers, symbolized by the three professors under the protective umbrella of the ubiquitous Vanstraaten Society; the other, a renewal of the author's efforts to recapture his early childhood—comprise a palpable attempt at a synthesis of the two styles. As such, the work expresses two distinct facets of Klaus Mann's artistic temperament: the first as revealed by the intensely lyrical outpourings of a lonely, uprooted youth, a perennial Kaspar Hauser, constantly at odds with an indifferent, at times hostile, world not of his own making; the second, that of a skeptical, at times despairing, social critic whose pessimistic appraisal of the political realities of his time borders on potentially fatal exaggeration. The consciously ''apocalyptic'' message of the play has clear political implications when one takes into account the author's mood and political stance at the time the work was written. Ideologically, the play bears a relation to Klaus Mann's problematical view of the uncertain world situation of 1945; structurally, it represents a reversion to his adolescent fantasy world of 1925.

If one disregards the political and autobiographical components of *The Seventh Angel*, it can still be interpreted purely and simply as a religious mystery play which incorporates the basic dual structure of traditional Christian eschatology. The philosophical and mythological base on which the play is founded has the structure of Manichaeism, which views the cosmos as a twofold entity, composed of an infinity of opposing forces, one part representing good, the other evil, where the Earth is seen as the testing ground on which the final outcome of the constant battle between these forces will be decided. While certain kinds of Christian dogma, however, teach that true faith will eventually bring about a happy resolution to the conflict, Klaus Mann leaves the final outcome in doubt. With love and good works, the impending catastrophe may be averted, but we are given no assurance that this will actually be the case. Instead, we are left with a clear admonition that we, rather than some external force, will be responsible for our own salvation.

V   *Other Post-War Writings*

The remainder of Klaus Mann's fiction written from the end of the Second World War until his death exists only in the form of outlines and sketches. With the exception of lyric poetry, all genres in which the author had previously been accustomed to working are represented. The outline of a play entitled *Simplicius*, loosely based on the novel *Simplicissimus* by Grimmelshausen, is yet another instance of the author's use of a historical source as a basis for illustrating a contemporary predicament. Although the manuscript itself is not dated, an allusion to the year 1945, as well as a provocative newspaper clipping citing the potential of the then recently developed atomic bomb for destroying the world are among the notes. Also present among Klaus's miscellaneous papers are some pessimistic statements from various historical sources calling attention to the unstable political situation which existed in Germany in the aftermath of the Thirty Years' War. His notes are also interspersed with somber pronouncements by known writers of the time such as Andreas Gryphius's "Es ist alles eitel" (All is [in] vain), all of which reflects Klaus's own mood at the time. Such background material leaves little doubt that he wanted to use the plot of *Simplicissimus* as a basis for communicating his own misgivings about a post-war situation which he perceived to be fraught with peril.

Although he wrote three separate outlines for the play, the last two do not radically differ from each other. His description of the first scene portrays an endless war with only brief and transitory respite, colored by an element of anti-Semitism, which helps to lend the play a contemporary air: "Mercenaries move through the city . . . plunder what is left to plunder . . . Want to kill the Jew . . . Simpl [icissimus] comes between them . . . Cries: 'The war is over.' Is laughed at at first, then insulted, beaten, locked up ('The war has lasted for thirty years: Why should it suddenly be over?')." (K. M. Archive) Despite his suffering, Simplicius—who is another variant of Kaspar Hauser—resolves to overcome his difficulties and, as is the case in the majority of Klaus Mann's works, begins to reconstruct his life in a spirit of hope and optimism. The final scene in each of the outlines depicts him about to rebuild his village with the words: "Es geht weiter" (Life continues), "Neubeginn" (New beginning) or "Von vorne anfangen" (Begin *ab ovo*).

The period commencing with Klaus's return to America and ending with his death in Cannes in the spring of 1949 seems to have been full of creative attempts which never came to fruition. A brief overview of his accomplishments during the last decade of his life and an optimistic prospectus outlining projects anticipated for the next decade begins with the heading, "The bad decade: 1939-48 . . . the beginning decade, 1949–58." It reveals the kind of ambivalent attitude toward his own abilities which is reflected in the personalities of many of the self-divided, youthful characters in his novels. A parenthetical remark appended to the section outlining "the beginning decade," which reads, "(if it has to be)" contains a hint of desperation about his future which is not evident in earlier statements about his plans and prospects. The list of his creative endeavors projected but never carried out contains the following description: "3 successful plays: One, sordid, morbid, sexy, bold and tragic; (one, in a light vein, maybe a historical comedy; one, fantastic, 'Traumspiel' [dream play], maybe utopian as with ghosts)." Along with his intention to expand his production of dramas in the tradition of *The Seventh Angel* he expresses a concomitant desire to write fewer articles and devote more of his energies to larger works of fiction and critical biographies similar to his study of Gide: "A booklet on Picasso; a quasi-philosophical monograph (Jakob Böhme?)." Also planned was a travel book, perhaps in the tradition of *Rundherum*, devoted to the Far East, principally China or India.

Among the works on the list on which Klaus Mann had begun working before his death are a homosexual novel, entitled *Windy Night, Rainy Morrow* and, psychologically perhaps the most revealing of all his works, a novel about political suicide entitled *The Last Day*. The former concerns two young men, Peter and Paul, who develop a homosexual relationship after Paul breaks his engagement with a well-to-do woman. In this aspect of the plot, Klaus may have been influenced by his own experience with Pamela Wedekind. A political element enters the novel when their relationship dissolves as a result of Peter's flirtation with Fascism and Paul's conversion to Communism. Peter becomes a successful film star while Paul is jailed as a consequence of his Communist sympathies. Because of the controversial nature of the subject matter, Klaus had intended to have the novel published under a pseudonym.

The Last Day, which contains the same basic plot structure as *Windy Night, Rainy Morrow*, centers on two young male characters who share similar, politically-motivated fates. It was in progress at the time of the author's death. A week-to-week schedule of chapters, appended to his notes, indicates that he was to have begun writing on the first of May, 1949, and to have finished all twenty chapters of the novel by the middle of August. The first chapter was almost completed, along with fragments of the thirteenth, seventeenth, nineteenth, and twentieth, which deal primarily with the planning and execution of the hero's suicide.

Briefly, the novel concerns the fate of Julian in New York and Albert in East Berlin, both captives, and eventually victims, of the turbulent political climate which existed at the beginning of the Cold War. Julian is a dedicated party-line Communist, driven to the point of despair over his inability to publish a vaunted "Manifesto" in a local Communist newspaper. Convinced of the futility of communicating his political message by conventional means, he hopes to draw sufficient public attention to his cause by staging a dramatic, politically motivated, suicide. Albert, in turn, becomes disillusioned by the oppressive political atmosphere of East Berlin and, in attempting to defect to the West, is brutally murdered by Communist agents.

The work is another attempt in the genre of the *Roman des*

Nebeneinander, except that, in this instance, the fates of the protagonists are played out independently of each other; and their paths never cross. The autobiographical elements characteristic of so many other Klaus Mann works are also included. Two minor characters, a female writer friend of Albert's named Paula Bertram and a friend of Julian's in New York, an English poet named Kenneth, are modelled after Anna Seghers and W. H. Auden, respectively. A third character, Dr. Kuno Sorge, "the nihilistic poet (old personal friend of Albert's), still in disgrace," is probably a caricature of Gottfried Benn. He asks Albert to intercede on his behalf in his attempt at denazification.

Taken in the context of Klaus Mann's own independent political position at the time, the novel is at once an intensive study of the motivation and technique for political suicide and an expression of the massive personal conflict which was raging deep within him in the weeks and months before his death. One of the fragments of the unfinished thirteenth chapter of the novel, in which Julian comes to the realization that the only solution to his problem is in suicide, contains a striking paralled to an essay entitled "Europe's Search for a New Credo," published a scant month after Klaus's death. The fragment reads:

The moral strength ensuing from absolute despair should be organized. A movement should be launched—the League of the Desperate Ones, the Hopelessness Society, The Suicide Club. The intellectual elite all over the world would join the organization— I don't know how they feel on the other side of the Iron Curtain, but in the Western world there would be considerable attendance . . . Individual acts of despair made an impression, but not enough. There was that German revolutionary poet who hung himself in a hotel room, not far from here, somewhere near Central Park . . . And the Austrian humanist who took his life in Brazil . . . The English novelist and *femme de lettres* who drowned herself—Ophelia-like . . . The Czech statesman jumping out of a window . . . Other examples . . . But those demonstrations ought to be coordinated . . . Then: I'd like to establish that club. But it would take too long . . . No time left . . . So how do I make the most of my personal tragedy . . ?' (K. M. Archive)

These thoughts are closely paraphrased in the conclusion of the posthumously published essay, in which Klaus ascribes them to a young Swedish student whom he claims to have met in his travels:

. . . the movement of despair, the rebellion of the hopeless ones. Instead of trying to appease the powers that be, instead of vindicating the machinations of greedy bankers or the outrages of tyrannical bureaucrats, we ought to go on record with our protest, with an unequivocal expression of our bitterness, our horror. Things have reached a point where only the most dramatic, most radical gesture has a chance to be noticed, to awaken the conscience of the blinded, hypnotized masses. I'd like to see hundreds, thousands of intellectuals follow the example of Virginia Woolf, Ernst Toller, Stefan Zweig, Jan Masaryk. A suicide wave among the world's most distinguished, most celebrated minds would shock the peoples out of their lethargy, would make them realize the extreme gravity of the ordeal man has brought upon himself by his folly and selfishness.[11]

Both declarations, one in an unfinished work of fiction, the other in an essay of socio-political criticism, coincide with their author's own suicide within weeks, perhaps even days, of the time in which they were written, to form the most dramatic and succinct example of how closely Klaus Mann's art had become representative of his life. Klaus left no suicide note in his hotel room in Cannes on the day of his death. There was no need of one. The writings which he left behind fully reveal his desperate wish to be heard, to call attention to the plight of a world which he genuinely believed to be on the brink of destruction. Much can be written about the political nature of his suicide and the various personal conflicts associated with the act. Richard Christ, in commenting on the extreme polarity in Klaus's attitude toward himself and the world in which he lived in the last years of his life, writes: "The tragedy of this clever and self-willed mind consisted in the fact that after the end of the war he remained without a historical compass and fell back into an isolation whose end point formed the theme of his essay 'Die Heimsuchung des Europäischen Geistes'; he himself took the consequence anticipated in the literary sphere and went the way of the 'Vulkan' figure, Martin Korella . . ."[12] The most compelling and immediate reasons for his suicide may never be known; but what comes to mind when one attempts to reconcile this final act of desperation with the total pattern of events in Klaus Mann's life is the recurring image of a homeless, wandering, uprooted young man, a twentieth-century Kaspar Hauser, in search of an identity, a new credo, who, finally convinced of the futility of his quest, finds his only permanent fulfillment in death.

CHAPTER 6

Summary

KLAUS Mann was, then, strongly motivated by youthful ideal-ism well beyond the earliest period in his career when his writings were devoted almost exclusively to problems associated with his own adolescence and youthful excesses. A close examination of his unpublished works written after 1939 shows that, with few exceptions, this formulation holds true for those works written during the last decade of his life as well. There are numerous reasons, conscious and unconscious, for his continued predilection for youth-oriented concerns, even as he was approaching middle age. In contrast to Thomas Mann, who had long maintained a deliberately apolitical, ironically detached posture, Klaus very early on felt constrained to assert himself as a proponent of political activism as a primary means of remedying the ills of contemporary society. As his political essays of the late 1920's and early 1930's demonstrate, he felt it incumbent upon himself and the members of his own generation to dissolve the narrow, misleading tenets of the parent generation and to strike out in new, bold and progressive directions, in order to correct the errors of the past which were again threatening to repeat themselves. He remained convinced that such a course of action would eventually usher in a new era of true stability, freedom, and enlightenment. This mandate, which assumed a sense of particular urgency in light of the rapidly deteriorating political situation of the 1930's, was shared by many of his contemporaries, but for Klaus it took on, with the passage of time, an increasing significance. Expressed in its simplest form, it was the assertion that the spirit of hope and the belief in progress which is almost universally associated with youth held the key to the survival of human institutions, and that his generation's failure to uphold its ideals would signal the doom of mankind.

The guiding principle of youth implicit in the vast majority of

131

Klaus Mann's writings throughout his career contains a basic ambivalence, most commonly associated with the searching, restless
nature of the adolescent who has not achieved the measure of stability and real fulfillment which is characteristic of mature adulthood. In Klaus Mann's case, this ambivalence was not limited to
the period of his own adolescent conflicts, which appear in disguised fashion throughout his early work, but continued to exert a
major formative influence on his later writings, up to the very end
of his life. The apodictic *either-or* which characterizes the final
chapter of *Der Wendepunkt* and forms part of the motivation of
his final suicide took its place in Klaus Mann's cosmology long before he swallowed the fatal dose of pills on that late spring day in
Cannes. An essay which he wrote in his middle twenties contains
the somber presentiments of an anonymous youthful critic, similar
to those in the final passage of *Die Heimsuchung des Europäischen
Geistes*: "In the astute essay of a young man I recently found the
alarming words: 'We, however, believe in the bad infinity, namely
in the fact that everything will always continue as at present and the
day will come on which we will be pushed into the darkest hell or
enter Paradise. *We stand at the eve of the gas war, in which Europe
will not fight itself, but destroy itself.* We, however, in our "peaceful disposition," don't believe it.' "[1] This statement, which Klaus
wrote in 1930, could easily have been transposed to 1949, with the
words "gas war" replaced by "nuclear war." The turbulent events
of two decades wrought little change in his basically ambivalent political posture; if they had any effect, it was to consolidate its negative aspect.

   In his role as political essayist and polemicist, Klaus Mann assumed the lifelong task of acting as spokesman and prophet for the
members of his generation and warning them of the imminence of
the choice which perpetually stood before them: hell or Paradise;
there was no in-between. Symptomatic of the conflict which fes-
tered within him increasingly during his last years, was his apparent
inability to come to grips with the fact that "the bad infinity,"
which had entered his consciousness in one form or another for
most of his adult life, is, for most people, merely an acknowledg-
ment of the unstable equilibrium which exists between human beings in an imperfect world. To the end, he evidently remained un-
willing to accept the notion that he, as an individual, could live suc-
cessfully, even happily, in a world where the solution to the prob-

lems of one generation engenders new ones in the next. Klaus's private, personal life eventually became so bound up with his concerns for humanity as a whole that the boundary line between the apocalyptic vision which had materialized in the last decade of his life and his own personal destiny became obscured, then finally eradicated.

In Klaus Mann's eyes, the precarious political balance between the opposing ideological forces of East and West, which had been a major precondition of the previous world wars, was threatening to form itself anew and to plunge the world eventually into a greater, more devastating conflict than the last. Embodied in the final, desperate plea of *Die Heimsuchung des Europäischen Geistes* is his firm conviction that the European intellectual, whom he had championed through all his mature years as the leading voice of reason and sanity in an otherwise chaotic world, had lost all ability to exert any meaningful influence on the course of human events. He did not live to see his prediction proved wrong. In the end, he seemed oblivious to the possibility of progress in a world in which the errors of the past were destined to repeat themselves eternally, and where there was no certainty that his vision of doom would not become a reality. In a mood much akin to that of a child who is angered by the broken promise of a trusted parent, he took his own life.

After an initial period of experimentation during the late 1920's, Klaus Mann began to develop a pattern in his fiction which combined the youthful characterizations in his early works with his new-found political consciousness of the 1930's. The works which he wrote from the beginning of his exile in 1933 until the beginning of the Second World War, and which constitute the bulk of his published fiction, show a predominance of youthful characters who seem, in many instances, to be carrying out the mandate which he set for himself and his contemporaries in his early political essays. One need only think of Jak, Gert, Johanna, Marcel Poiret and others to realize that the major part of Klaus Mann's work is dedicated to the kind of political *engagement* which he genuinely felt was necessary to turn the tide of world events. Even his relatively early *Alexander* is a parodistic attempt to combine the traits of a great historical individual with the more mundane characteristics of a twentieth-century Pan-Europeanist. One need also not delve very deeply into the plot structure of Klaus Mann's total *oeuvre* to observe that most of these young, idealistic characters eventually fail in their tasks, many at the cost of their lives, if not of their ultimate happiness. It is as though some unseen mechanism operated beneath his consciousness which required him to create characters whose potential for self-destruction is at least as great as their capacity for constructive self-realization. Of even greater importance, psychologically, is the fact that the author's own mood and activities closely parallel those of a number of his key characters; the low self-esteem which is typical of many of his morbidly fatalistic, sometimes suicidal figures was undoubtedly shared by Klaus himself, not only toward the end of his life, but in the earlier stages of his career as well. It is no coincidence, for instance, that the relatively minor character, Richard Darmstädter, of *Treffpunkt im Unendlichen*, who bears numerous other similarities to the author, commits suicide in much the same manner as Klaus Mann himself, many years after the novel was written.

Klaus Mann's lifelong tendency to weave characterizations and experiences from his life into the fabric of his fiction began early in his career, before he had made up his mind to become a professional writer. Kaspar Hauser, the prototype for many of the central characters in works which represent every phase of his life, was incorporated into his early work and even then acknowledged to have an almost mystical significance for him. The term *Kaspar-Hauser-Complex*, mentioned, but not elaborated upon by Klaus in relation to some of his earliest writings, has implications which transcend the appearance of any one character in a particular work. Close examination of his later work shows that it can serve as a model for any number of different character types and patterns of behavior which appear in various stages of his career.

Most of the central characters in Klaus Mann's fiction are endowed with an excess of zeal and creative energy, which in many instances is sublimated into either artistic endeavors—in the early work—or political activism—in the literature of the emigration; only rarely are the individuals brought to a point of permanent stability in their lives. Such a state of perpetual unrest is most characteristic of the adolescent stage of human development, normally a transitional period, during which the individual systematically tests out and discards the patterns of behavior which served him well as a child, but are inappropriate to the adult. As such, the character of Kaspar Hauser, the foundling of Nuremberg, is a fitting symbol for the kind of adolescent mode of existence which Klaus Mann sought to depict in his youthful writings. In his most pristine representation, the central character of the *Kaspar Hauser Legenden* is a universal image, the melancholy young wanderer, in futile quest of the mother and sister who comprise the vestiges of an idyllic childhood which is no longer accessible to him. Peculiar to most of Klaus Mann's characters in every stage of his career, and particularly significant for his artistic and psychological development, however, is the fact that his characters are for the most part fixed in this interim phase of their own development and rarely work through their adolescent conflicts. They seem permanently incapable of transcending the limitations of the *Kaspar-Hauser-Complex* and becoming mature, autonomous adults, prepared to live in relative peace and security in an imperfect world.

The transition which Klaus had to make between such works as *Anja und Esther* and *Kindernovelle* and the works for which he is best known, the novels of emigration, was relatively simple because he had only to place the youthful, searching characters of the fiction of his own youth into the more topical historical and cultural milieu of the 1930's. His first novel, *Der fromme Tanz*, although written several years before the Nazi period, bears numerous structural and stylistic similarities to his last and most ambitious published novel, *Der Vulkan*. With few exceptions, the novels representing the chronological center between these two extremes, which include *Treffpunkt im Unendlichen* and *Flucht in den Norden*, incorporate a basic motif which is also central to the *Kaspar-Hauser-Complex*, that of *flight*. Even such disparate and atypical novels as *Symphonie Pathétique* and *Mephisto* are built around main characters who are not emigrants in a literal sense but who are caught up in a kind of psychological emigration which makes them constantly attempt to flee their own inner conflicts. In the works in which the historical emigration plays a manifest role, the theme of flight is no longer associated with rebellion from parental authority, as it is in the very early works, but becomes bound up with the characters' political ideologies, which are commensurate with the uncertain and changing political configurations of Europe in the 1930's. Thus, Klaus Mann was easily able to retain the theme of flight as a basic structural element in his fiction while altering the subject matter to conform to the radically changing conditions in the world and in his own life.

For Klaus Mann, suicide is the ultimate form of flight. On occasions where his protagonists find release neither in political activity nor in the possibility of sensual fulfillment, they choose suicide as the final solution to their problems. The genesis of this particular motivational complex and be found in the short story, *Letztes Gespräch*, which contains the same basic conflict as *Flucht in den Norden*, but has a less fortunate resolution. Although the reasons for each of the many suicides depicted in Klaus Mann's work are complex and unique to each individual instance, political factors are associated with many of them. Since the majority of his characters suffer from strong feelings of inadequacy which manifest themselves in the frustration of their utopian ambitions and their inability to find a suitable alternative activity through which they might more realistically fulfill themselves, suicide appears to be the only course left open to them.

Aside from the pattern of suicidal motifs which occurs in every phase of Klaus Mann's work, there are numerous instances in which other clearly demonstrable autobiographical elements appear with regularity in his fiction. It is impossible to assess with certainty the extent to which a given writer relies on his present and past experiences to stimulate his imagination to the point where the creative process begins; all writers draw to some degree from the world around them in order to form the basis on which to apply their creative fantasy and ultimately to construct an independent work of art. Klaus Mann's fiction, however, in every stage of its development, displays an unusually heavy reliance on people and events in his day-to-day experience to form characters and situations whose genesis cannot be explained solely by virtue of artistic design. The strong empathy between the author and a large number of his characters who bear some resemblance to himself or to persons of his acquaintance lends credence to the assertion that the totality of his work, when viewed both from a critical and a historical perspective, contains the skeleton of a largely unconscious autobiography, whose basic structure remained hidden even to the author himself.

His final work, intended to be an in-depth psychological study of political suicide, but which became instead his most definitive statement of his own intentions and his most articulate epitaph,[2] was but the last and most dramatically apparent instance in a long series of partially disguised fantasies and self-portraits which had been integrated into the mosaic of his entire work. The youthful image of the restless, dissatisfied Prince Kaspar, attempting, in his own characteristic way, to escape the oppressive yoke of "a strict and decorous monarch," is but a single, early representation of one of the real life situations in which the young Klaus Mann envisioned himself. The fact that he, too, left the paternal home early in life and led the life of a virtual exile, even before the course of world events forced him into actually becoming one, and the fact that he never really found a permanent home or a satisfying *modus vivendi* are largely the result of forces within his mind which remained beyond his conscious control and are documented in the life situations of the vast majority of his characters, to whom flight and perpetual exile are a constant way of life.

The influence which Thomas Mann had in his son's life and work is of enormous significance. Although Klaus made a deliberate attempt to minimize the effect of his father's writing on the development of his own style and literary interests, the mere fact that he was the son of a world-renowned writer was a burden which he had to bear silently all his life. It was doubtless also an important factor in the depression which eventually caused him to terminate his life. While it is true that Klaus was never able to convince himself that whatever reputation he gained as a writer was not in part due to the fact that he was the son of Thomas Mann, the actual product of his creative efforts bears scant resemblance to that of his father. Klaus's mature fiction contains little of the ironic, detached intellectuality for which Thomas Mann is so well known; the intensity and earnest pathos with which the heroes of *Der Vulkan* confront their problems stand in sharp contrast to the cool insularity of the characters in *The Magic Mountain*. It must also be remembered that Klaus earned his livelihood as a freelance journalist and essayist, not solely as a writer of fiction. Although all his life he doubtless wanted to gain a reputation as a novelist on a par with that of his father, his critical and editorial pursuits alone testify to his intellectual and professional independence.

To characterize all of Klaus Mann's fiction as either youthful polemicizing or veiled autobiography, however, would not only be an oversimplification of the facts, but also an unrealistic appraisal of its overall artistic worth. Klaus wrote a number of works which deal with characters who are neither youthful nor politically motivated, some of which must be counted among his best efforts. The novella *Vergittertes Fenster*, whose importance was unjustly over-shadowed by the equally atypical and controversial *Mephisto* which happened to appear a scant year earlier, is a first-rate study of the inner workings of a mind in the process of being destroyed by mad-ness. As such, it bears only superficial resemblance to the bulk of the works which appeared earlier or were written subsequently. Similarly, the novels which treat the lives of other historical figures who had a special meaning for Klaus Mann must be placed in a unique category when his total work is taken into perspective.

Finally, his autobiographies, *Kind dieser Zeit* and *Der Wende-punkt*, are as much documents of our time as chronicles of the au-thor's experience. While they present us with a detailed account of his relations with an array of well-and lesser-known individuals, in addition to a few glimpses into his private life, their primary impor-tance lies in the fact that they review an important period of our history from a unique perspective. Klaus Mann did, indeed, repre-sent the view of the young European intellectual between the two World Wars; as is often the case with highly sensitive, prophetic individuals who attempt to raise their voices above the din of ordi-nary human discourse, he could never be certain that he was truly being heard.

Notes and References

Page references to quotations from Klaus Mann's works appear parenthetically after each quotation. In the case of works which have been reprinted, the references are to the latest editions. All translations are by the author of this monograph. Quotations from works originally written in English by Klaus Mann and others are given in the original.

Chapter One

1. Klaus Mann, *Kind dieser Zeit* (Munich: Nymphenburger, 1956), p. 256.
2. Klaus Mann, *Der Wendepunkt* (Munich: Nymphenburger, 1969), pp. 240-44.
3. As late as 1966, a lawsuit was instituted in an attempt to prevent publication of *Mephisto* in West Germany. See Willi Köhler, "Politisches Buchverbot" in *Neue Deutsche Literatur*, 14, No. 4 (1966), p. 18.
4. Golo Mann, "Erinnerungen an meinen Bruder Klaus" in Martin Gregor-Dellin, ed., *Klaus Mann. Briefe und Antworten*, II, (Munich: Nymphenburger, 1975), p. 343.

Chapter Two

1. *Kind dieser Zeit*, pp. 32-33.
2. See *Der Wendepunkt*, pp. 181 ff.
3. Erika Mann, ed., *Klaus Mann zum Gedächtnis* (Amsterdam: Querido, 1950), p. 9.
4. *Ibid.*, p. 133.
5. From this writer's conversation with Peter de Mendelssohn on October 5, 1972. He and Klaus had been close friends from the time they both attended the *Odenwaldschule*.
6. An accurate, if somewhat playful portrayal of Klaus in this particular phase of his life is given in Thomas Mann's short story, *Unordnung und frühes Leid* (Disorder and Early Sorrow).

7. Which, in addition to Pamela, consisted of W. E. Süskind, a young man-about-town named Theo, and Klaus's childhood friend Ricki Hallgarten, whose suicide was to have a strong impact on Klaus less than a decade later. Erika was also included in this group.

Chapter Three

1. Not to be confused with his early short story described in the previous chapter, which will henceforth be referred to as "Vor dem Leben I."

2. Jakob Wassermann, *Caspar Hauser oder die Trägheit des Herzens* (Berlin: S. Fischer, 1908), p. 557.

3. Klaus Mann, "Kaspar Hauser," *Die Weltbühne* 21 (June, 1925), p. 511.

4. Klaus Mann, *The Turning Point* (New York: L. B. Fischer, 1942), p. 107.

5. This feeling was conveyed to the writer in conversations with his youngest brother, Michael, and his mother, Katja Mann.

6. Klaus Mann, "Heute und Morgen" in *Auf der Suche nach einem Weg* (Berlin: Transmare, 1931), p. 25.

7. For a more detailed justification by Klaus Mann for using America as a background for a play about anti-intellectualism, see "Die Jugend und Paneuropa" in *Suche*, pp. 73 ff.

8. The others: *Symphonie Pathétique* (1935) and *Vergittertes Fenster* (1937).

Chapter Four

1. The play which Klaus refers to here is *Geschwister* (Siblings), a dramatic reworking of Jean Cocteau's novel, *Les Enfants Terribles*.

2. For a detailed discussion of Gründgens' relation to Klaus Mann's work, see Werner Rieck, "Gregor Gregori und Hendrik Höfgen (Ein Beitrag zur Werkgeschichte von Klaus Manns 'Mephisto')" in *Pädagogische Hochschule Potsdam, Wissenschaftliche Zeitschrift*, 12, No. 5 (1968), pp. 697-709; and id. "Zur Genesis einer Romanfigur von Klaus Mann" in *Weimarer Beiträge*, 15 (1969), pp. 855-70.

3. See Klaus Mann, *Treffpunkt im Unendlichen* (Berlin: S. Fischer, 1932), pp. 213-220.

4. *Wendepunkt*, pp. 240-44.

5. *Ibid.*, p. 332. The Persian trip was to have taken place in May, 1932, but had to be cancelled because of Hallgarten's suicide.

6. Christopher Isherwood, *Exhumations* (New York: Simon and Schuster, 1966), p. 137.

7. Klaus Mann, "Letztes Gespräch" in *Die Sammlung: Literarische Monatsschrift unter dem Patronat von André Gide, Aldous Huxley, und Heinrich Mann*, vol. 1, No. 6 (1934), p. 303.

8. Quoted in Günter Hartung, "Klaus Manns Zeitschrift 'Die Sammlung' (Teil I)," *Weimarer Beiträge*, 19, No. 5 (1967), p. 46.

9. Quoted in Hans-Albert Walter, "Der Streit um 'Die Sammlung,' " *Frankfurter Hefte*, 21 (1966), p. 852.

10. *Ibid.*, p. 854.

11. *Klaus Mann. Briefe und Antworten*, I, p. 137.

12. *Ibid.*, p. 134.

13. Whether the historical Tchaikovsky was, in fact, homosexual is open to question. It is, however, characteristic of Klaus Mann to portray many of his characters, whether based on historical individuals or not, as homosexuals.

14. Klaus Mann, "Kein Schlüsselroman" in Martin Gregor-Dellin, ed., *Klaus Mann: Die Heimsuchung des Europäischen Geistes. Aufsätze* (Munich: Deutscher Taschenbuch Verlag, 1973), p. 40.

15. This suggests that Klaus's tendency to model his characters on real individuals found its first practical application here as a political device, whereas previously it had served only an artistic purpose.

16. See above, *Introduction*, note 3.

17. Fritz Strich, *Kunst und Leben* (Berne: Franke, 1960), p. 198. The term is originally attributed to Gutzkow.

18. See Golo Mann, "Erinnerungen an meinen Bruder Klaus" in *Briefe und Antworten*, II, pp. 330-31.

19. Martin Gregor-Dellin, "Klaus Mann und seine Generation," *Neue deutsche Hefte*, 26, No. 2 (1969), p. 55.

Chapter Five

1. The original manuscript of this and other unpublished stories of Klaus Mann cited in this chapter can be found in the Klaus Mann Archive in the *Handschriftensammlung* of the *Stadtbibliothek München*.

2. Klaus Mann, "Le Dernier Cri," *Esquire*, 15 (May, 1941), p. 147.

3. *Ibid.*, p. 150.

4. *Decision. A Review of Free Culture*, 1, 1 (1941), p. 7.

5. *Briefe und Antworten*, II, p. 164.

6. *Ibid.*, p. 165.

7. *Ibid.*, p. 178.

8. See *The Other Germany* (New York: Modern Age, 1940), p. 148.

9. *Der siebente Engel, TS,* (Zurich: Oprecht, 1946), p. 92.

10. As in the Mann family, there are six children: starting with the youngest, a boy; then two girls; two boys; and a girl. It should be recalled

that in the period in Klaus's life which *Kindernovelle* is meant to represent the two youngest Mann siblings, Michael and Elisabeth, had not yet been born.

11. Klaus Mann, "Europe's Search for a New Credo," *Tomorrow*, 8, No. 10 (June 1949), p. 11. The essay was subsequently translated by Erika Mann and published as *Die Heimsuchung des europäischen Geistes* (The Ordeal of the European Spirit), in the volume *Klaus Mann zum Gedächtnis*.

12. Richard Christ, "Das unausweichliche Entweder-Oder!" *Neue Deutsche Literatur,* 18 (1970), p. 172.

Chapter Six

1. Klaus Mann, "Zur Situation" in *Auf der Suche nach einem Weg* (Berlin: Transmare, 1931), p. 85.

2. The following verse from *Luke* (IX: 24), frequently cited in Klaus's biography of Gide, is engraved on his tombstone: "For whosoever will save his life shall lose it; but whosoever will lose his life . . . the same shall find it." It was also intended to be used as a motto for *The Last Day.*

Selected Bibliography

PRIMARY SOURCES

1. Books (in chronological order):
Vor dem Leben. Erzählungen. Hamburg: Gebrüder Enoch, 1925.
Anja und Esther. Romantisches Stück. Berlin: Oesterheld, 1925.
Der fromme Tanz. Das Abenteuerbuch einer Jugend. Hamburg: Gebrüder Enoch, 1926.
Kindernovelle. 1926; rpt. Munich: Nymphenburger Verlagshandlung, 1964.
Rundherum (with Erika Mann). Berlin: S. Fischer, 1929.
Abenteuer. Novellen. Leipzig: Philipp Reclam jun., 1929.
Gegenüber von China. Komödie. TS, Berlin: Oesterheld, 1929.
Alexander. Roman der Utopie. 1930; rpt. Munich: Nymphenburger Verlagshandlung, 1963.
Auf der Suche nach einem Weg. Aufsätze. Berlin: Transmare Verlag, 1931.
Kind dieser Zeit. 1932; rpt. Munich: Nymphenburger Verlagshandlung, 1965.
Treffpunkt im Unendlichen. Roman. Berlin: S. Fischer, 1932.
Flucht in den Norden. Roman. Amsterdam: Querido, 1934.
Symphonie Pathétique. Ein Tschaikowsky-Roman. 1935; rpt. Munich: Nymphenburger Verlagshandlung, 1970.
Mephisto. Roman einer Karriere. 1936; rpt. Munich: Nymphenburger Verlagshandlung, 1965.
Vergittertes Fenster. Novelle um den Tod des Königs Ludwig II. von Bayern. 1937; rpt. Munich: Nymphenburger Verlagshandlung, 1972.
Der Vulkan. Roman unter Emigranten. 1939; rpt. Munich: Nymphenburger Verlagshandlung, 1968.
Escape to Life (with Erika Mann). Boston: Houghton Mifflin and Co., 1939.
The Other Germany (with Erika Mann). New York: Modern Age Books, 1940.
The Turning Point. Thirty-five years in this century. New York: L. B. Fischer, 1942.

André Gide and the Crisis of Modern Thought. New York: Creative Age
        Press, 1943.

Der siebente Engel. TS. Zurich: Europa-Verlag, 1946.

Der Wendepunkt. Ein Lebensbericht. Munich: Nymphenburger Verlags-
        handlung, 1969.

Prüfungen. Schriften zur Literatur. ed. Martin Gregor-Dellin. Munich:
        Nymphenburger Verlagshandlung, 1968.

Heute und Morgen. Schriften zur Zeit. ed. Martin Gregor-Dellin. Munich:
        Nymphenburger Verlagshandlung, 1969.

2. Short Works in Periodicals (in chronological order):

"Traum des verlorenen Sohnes von der Heimkehr." *Vossiche Zeitung*,
        March 17, 1925.

"Kaspar Hauser." *Die Weltbühne*, 21 (June 1925), 511-12.

"Letztes Gespräch." *Die Sammlung*, 1, No. 6 (Feb. 1934), 297-305.

"My Father's Political Development." *Common Sense*, 6, No. 2 (Feb.
        1937), 8-10.

"Le Dernier Cri." *Esquire*, 15 (May 1941), 28 ff.

"Europe's Search for a New Credo." *Tomorrow*, 8, No 10 (June 1949), 5-
        11.

3. Unpublished Manuscripts (in chronological order):

Nach der Sintflut. Outline of a Novel, c. 1937.

Speed: A Story, Aug./Sept., 1940.

"Three Star Hennessy." Story, c. 1940.

"The Monk." Story, 1943.

The Dead Don't Care. Play in Three Acts, 1943.

Ghosts. Outline of a Novel, 1943.

A Book on Postwar Germany. Outline, 1945.

Simplicius. Sketches for a Play, c. 1945.

House Hollberg. Fragment of a Play, c. 1945.

Fräulein. Sketches and Outline for a Novel, c. 1947.

The Bad Decade 1939-1948; The Beginning Decade, (If It Has to Be!).
        Outline, 1949.

The Last Day. Fragment of a Novel, 1949.

4. Letters:

Klaus Mann. Briefe und Antworten. ed. Martin Gregor-Dellin. 2 vols.
        Munich: Ellermann, 1975.

5. English Translations:

The Fifth Child. tr. Lambert Armour Shears. New York: Boni and
        Liveright, 1927.

Alexander. tr. Marion Saunders. New York: Brewer and Warren, 1930.

Journey into Freedom. tr. Rita Reil. London: Gollancz, 1936; New York: Knopf, 1936.

Pathetic Symphony: A Tchaikovsky Novel. tr. Herman Ould. London: Gollancz, 1938.

Pathetic Symphony: A Novel about Tchaikovsky. New York: Allen, Towne and Heath, 1948.

SECONDARY SOURCES

1. Books:

BADEN, HANS JÜRGEN. *Literature und Selbstmord*. Stuttgart: Klett, 1965. Contains an analysis of suicidal motives in Klaus Mann's life and work.

DIRSCHAUER, WILFRIED. *Klaus Mann und das Exil*. Worms: Georg Heintz, 1973. Comprehensive analysis of Klaus Mann's political views.

ISHERWOOD, CHRISTOPHER. *Exhumations*. New York: Simon and Schuster, 1966. Contains a sensitive memoir of Klaus Mann by an old friend.

MANN, ERIKA, ed. *Klaus Mann zum Gedächtnis*. Amsterdam: Querido, 1950. A collection of eulogies and reminiscences by a number of Klaus Mann's friends and acquaintances, published shortly after his death.

REICH—RANICKI, MARCEL. *Die Ungeliebten: Sieben Emigranten*. Pfullingen: Neske, 1968. Contains a perceptive analysis of the relationship between Klaus Mann and Gustaf Gründgens and its bearing on the *Mephisto* controversy.

STRICH, FRITZ. *Kunst und Leben. Vorträge und Abhandlungen zur deutschen Kultur*. Berne: Francke, 1960.

WEGNER, MATTHIAS. *Exil und Literatur. Deutsche Schriftsteller im Ausland*. Frankfurt a/M and Bonn: Athenäum Verlag, 1967. Survey of the work of German writers in exile. Contains a fairly detailed analysis of *Der Vulkan*.

2. Dissertations: (unpublished)

HARRISON, EVERETT FALCONER. "Death and Decadence in the Works of Klaus Mann," Harvard, 1967.

KROLL, FREDERIC JOSEPH. "Klaus Mann und die Synthese von Moral und Schönheit," Rochester, 1973. Contains the most complete bibliography of Klaus Mann's work to date.

3. Articles:

BERENDSOHN, WALTER. "Klaus Manns Autobiographie 'Der Wendepunkt'," *Moderna Sproak*, 64 (1970), 252-57.

CHRIST, RICHARD. "Das unausweichliche Entweder-Oder," *Neue Deutsche Literatur*, 18 (1970), 167-72. In-depth analysis of *Der Vulkan*.

GREGOR—DELLIN, MARTIN. "Klaus Mann und seine Generation," *Neue deutsche Hefte*, 26, No 2 (1969), 47-64. Brief overview of Klaus Mann's life and work by the editor of the most recent editions of his works.

GROSSHUT, F. S. "Death of a Writer," *Commentary*, 9 (June 1950), 553-55. Relates Klaus Mann's suicide to the refusal of a German publisher (Georg Jacobi) to reprint *Mephisto*.

HARTUNG, GÜNTER. "Klaus Manns Zeitschrift 'Die Sammlung' (Teil I)," *Weimarer Beiträge*, 29, No. 5 (1967), 37-59.

———————————— "Klaus Manns Zeitschrift 'Die Sammlung' (Teil II)," *Weimarer Beiträge*, 19, No. 6 (1967), 95-117. Thorough analysis of the controversy surrounding the publication of Klaus Mann's first journal.

KESTEN, HERMANN. "Klaus Mann," *Neue Rundschau. Berlin*, (1949), 573-80. Reminiscences by an old friend and colleague.

RIECK, WERNER. "Gregor Gregori und Hendrik Höfgen (Ein Beitrag zur Werkgeschichte von Klaus Manns 'Mephisto')," *Pädagogische Hochschule Potsdam Wissenschaftliche Zeitschrift*, 12, No. 5 (1968), 697-709.

———————————— "Zur Genesis einer Romanfigur von Klaus Mann," *Weimarer Beiträge*, 15 (1969), 855-70. Both of the above treat the relationship between characters in *Treffpunkt im Unendlichen* and *Mephisto* and living persons, with special emphasis on Gustaf Gründgens.

SCHNEIDER, ROLF. "Klaus Mann," *Aufbau*, 12 (1956), 1105-19. Brief but probing analysis of Klaus Mann's life and work.

WALTER, HANS-ALBERT. "Der Streit um 'Die Sammlung'," *Frankfurter Hefte*, 21 (1966), 850-60.

———————————— "Klaus Mann und 'Die Sammlung'," *Frankfurter Hefte*, 22 (1967), 49-58.

Index